Missionary Chronicles

AMBASSADOR PUBLICATIONS
Minneapolis, Minnesota

MISSIONARY CHRONICLES

© 2008 Ambassador Publications
Board of Publications and Parish Education
Association of Free Lutheran Congregations (AFLC)
3110 East Medicine Lake Boulevard
Minneapolis, MN 55441

Scripture taken from the NEW AMERICAN STANDARD BIBLE®,
©Copyright The Lockman Foundation 1960, 1962, 1963, 1968, 1971, 1972, 1973, 1975, 1977, 1995. Used by permission.

All rights reserved. No part of this book may be reproduced or transmitted in any form or by any means, electronic or mechanical, including photocopying, recording, or by any information storage and retrieval system, without permission in writing from the publisher.

ISBN 9781585720705
Library of Congress Control Number: 2008928391

PRINTED IN THE UNITED STATES OF AMERICA

Table of Contents

Preface — v
Foreword — vii
Introduction — ix

Africa

The Tree That Withered Away	Amos O. Dyrud	3
"Almost Persuaded"	Amos O. Dyrud	8
A Bell Rings for Koroline	Amos O. Dyrud	14
More Powerful Than Satan	Rachel Chesley	18
Bernincha's Bracelet	Rachel Chesley	22
Tabletop Appendectomy	Jerry and Maija Carlson	26
Eagle Wings to the Rescue	Jerry and Maija Carlson	30
Fire! Fire!	Elaine Kohl	35
Sowing in Sorrow, Reaping in Joy	Inez Eikom	39
Jonathan and the Little Black Book	Rhoda Jore	43
A Visit to Bukoma	Del Palmer	48
In the Middle of Nowhere	Kevin Olson	52

Hymn: "Dear Savior, Bless the Children" — 56
Hymn: "Savior, While My Heart Is Tender" — 57

Asia

The Fields Are White . . .	Jerome Elness	59
Who Lives in Your House?	Eugene Enderlein	62
God's Love in Colors	Karen Palmer	66
A New Song in an Old Country	Don Richman	70

Hymn: "O Zion, Haste" — 74
Hymn: "We've a Story to Tell to the Nations" — 75

Europe

Babushka's Prayer	Ellen Monseth	77
Iwona's Mountaintop Mission	Tim Hinrichs	80

Hymn: "I Love to Tell the Story" — 84

North America

"What Can *I* Do?"	Clara Gunderson	87
"Nothing Shall Hurt You"	Linda Haabak	90
Border Crossing	Todd Schierkolk	93
Mario and Viki	Todd Schierkolk	97
A New Life for Virginia	MaryAnn Jackson	101
"We Are Praying for You"	Karen Knudsvig	105
Phone Calls from God?	Tom Olson	110
The Hands That Speak	Linda Mohagen	115
Flight Plan	Lori Willard	119
A Mother's Goodbye	Ellen Monseth	124

Hymn: "Hail to the Brightness"   127

South America

Snapshots	Ruby Abel	129
"Snakes!"	Ruby Abel	133
Bruno	John Abel	136
Nida	Alvin Grothe	140
Promises for Dulcé	Helen and Carol Knapp	144
Precila's "Mansion"	Connely Dyrud	149
"Why Was I Born Here?"	Connely Dyrud	155
Under the Southern Cross	Loiell Dyrud	160
A Fisher of Men	Becky Abel	165
Freedom from Bondage	Becky Abel	169
Fighting Willy	Jonathan Abel	173
Looking for Hope	Tamba Abel	177
Miracle on the Mountain	Dan Giles	181
Irma, God's Messenger of Contentment	Richard Gunderson	185
Christmas in Bolivia	Clara Gunderson	189

Appendixes

Appendix A — Pronunciation Key	193
Appendix B — Story Illustrators	194
Appendix C — Teaching Missions to Children	196

Preface

As a child growing up in a Christian home, my parents often hosted missionaries who were visiting our church while they were home on furlough. I loved to sit at the table and listen to the stories they told about the places where they were ministering. The adventure and excitement of living in a foreign country, learning another language, and adapting to a different culture were intriguing. As an adult, I still enjoy hearing about the work of our missionaries.

Because the Women's Missionary Federation (WMF) of the AFLC is a missionary-supporting organization, we have endeavored to encourage and pray for the AFLC Board of Publications and Parish Education in putting together this missionary story book. It is with great joy that the WMF has also given monetary gifts toward its publication so that we can read accounts of missionary experiences.

God has blessed our AFLC with men and women who have felt the call to serve the Lord in missions. We pray that this book will encourage people of all ages to be open to God's call to be involved in mission work.

Mrs. Lorilee Mundfrom   April 2008
President of the Women's Missionary Federation
Association of Free Lutheran Congregations (AFLC)

Foreword

The work God is doing through our missionaries happens far away and often far removed from our sight. However, because *Missionary Chronicles* is written as a series of short stories, this book provides a direct connection between reader and missionary. The next time a missionary with a story in this volume visits your congregation, a bond will already exist because part of the missionary's life and ministry has been revealed through one of these stories.

Children love to have someone read to them. Next to reading them the Word of God, nothing could be better than reading your children testimonies of God working through the lives of men and women of faith. These stories build faith as children hear God's promises and see how He works in the personal lives of these missionaries. The situations we read about here teach children how to share their faith and how to live their lives, walking with the Savior.

Read one of the stories from this book as a family each night before bed. Use one story each week for opening chapel time in Sunday School or at a youth meeting or adult Bible study. Then talk about the story. Allow God to speak to you about praying for missions, giving to missions, and even serving as a foreign missionary. Only eternity will reveal the blessings of our prayers, gifts, and service to the Lord.

Ambassador Publications has provided a great service for the AFLC by placing this book in our hands. The stories in this book are written by AFLC missionaries and by missionaries with connections to the AFLC and are a compilation of real-life mission experiences that can now be shared with our children and grandchildren.

I pray that this book will be a rich blessing to you and your family, not only as you read about missionaries and their work, but also as God challenges you to walk wholeheartedly with Him.

Rev. Del Palmer   April 2008
Director of World Missions
Minneapolis, Minnesota

Introduction

Missionaries often came to our church to show slides and tell about their work while I was growing up. Their pictures were posted on the church bulletin board, and we heard their names frequently. We also had a monthly mission club for elementary age children. There we would hear mission stories and sing mission songs, read letters from missionaries, sign birthday cards to send to them and their families, participate in mission projects, and pray for missionaries. We also regularly prayed for missionaries by name in our home.

Teaching about missions is an essential part of Christian education in the congregation and in the home. Children should be taught from a young age to have *beautiful feet*. "How then will they call on Him in whom they have not believed? How will they believe in Him whom they have not heard? And how will they hear without a preacher? How will they preach unless they are sent? Just as it is written, 'HOW BEAUTIFUL ARE THE FEET OF THOSE WHO BRING GOOD NEWS OF GOOD THINGS!'"(Romans 10:14-15).

In the fall of 2000, Ambassador Publications decided that publishing a book of mission stories would be a valuable tool for teaching children about missions. A notice was posted in *The Lutheran Ambassador* inviting people to send mission stories to our office to be compiled in a collection of short stories. The invitation was open to anyone connected with an AFLC congregation who either currently or previously served on a foreign field through any mission organization, whether short-term or long-term. Personal letters were also sent to a large number of people, inviting them to participate in this project. Only a few stories were received at that time. Through public notices, letters, and phone calls, we continued encouraging people to submit stories about their mission experiences. People always seemed excited about the idea when it was presented, but only a few more stories trickled into our office during the next few years.

In 2003 the Board of Publications decided that in order to move forward, we needed an individual who could commit a large amount of time to the project and take it on as a personal ministry opportunity. This person would be responsible for making contacts with prospective writers, seeking commitments from them to submit one or more stories, and regularly following up on their work. The board approached former missionary, Mrs. Clara Gunderson, about this task, and she willingly consented to serve. We are grateful to Clara for her humble service and for the extensive work she has done, communicating regularly with writers and helping them put their accounts into an interesting story form with active dialogue and vivid details. Thanks also to Mrs. Fern Bohling and Mr. Loiell Dyrud, who have given valuable assistance in this enormous task. We are also grateful to the Women's Missionary Federation (WMF), who has always been a key supporter and promoter of mission work and has encouraged this project from the beginning, generously providing funding for it.

The forty-three stories that make up *Missionary Chronicles* reflect God's work in mission endeavors on five continents. The included maps are intended to give geographical context to the stories they represent. The story illustrators range in age from four to seventeen. A series of discussion questions follows each story, along with a brief biographical sketch about each writer. Also included are creative ideas for teaching missions to children and several hymns with a missions focus.

The goals of the book are to create an awareness of mission work around the world, to awaken an interest in missions (especially of AFLC missions), and to encourage people to pray for missionaries, give to missions, and consider God's personal calling to missions both at home and abroad. This collection of short stories is intended to be a helpful resource for family devotions, opening chapel time, or Sunday School classrooms.

Many of these stories in faraway lands describe adventures unlike the typical American experience. Yet the timeless truths they teach are not bound by the location or age level of the reader. The varied stories give a realistic picture of the missionary experience. They tell about the call to missions, painful separation of loved ones, difficult circumstances, disappointments, and rejection of the Gospel, but they also show God at work on the mission field through answered prayers, God's provision and protection, and the salvation of souls. May God use this book to awaken in our hearts a desire to bring the wonderful words of the Gospel to our own communities and to the remotest parts of the earth.

Mrs. Marian Christopherson May 2008
Director of Publications and Parish Education
Minneapolis, Minnesota

Missionary Chronicles

Africa

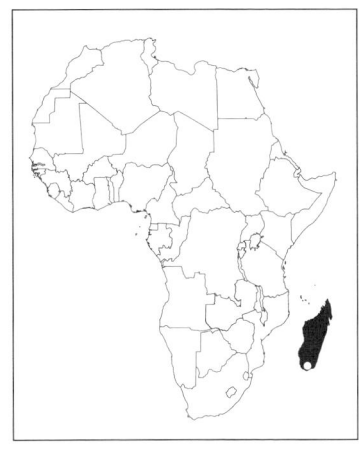

The Tree That Withered Away

By Amos O. Dyrud
(as told to Loiell Dyrud)

"A-ough! A-ough!" Adolphe Santinely (SAHNT-ah-NEL-ee) heard it again. It was the sound of someone coughing outside his door. But he was in prayer, and the owner of the house, Andre, was not home. Adolphe ignored the disturbance. "A-ough! A-ough! A-ough!" Realizing whoever was at the door was not going away, Adolphe relented and opened the door.

"Did you want Andre? He's not here right now," he said. It was a woman he had not seen before in Votovoatavo (voh-toh-vah-TAH-voh).

"My name is Kalovary (kahl-ah-VAHR-ee)," she said shyly, "I live in Behera (bay-HAR-ah) about two hours away. I came here because I heard about the meetings you were having. I was told I could find you in this house. They said you and *ny vazaha* (the foreigner) are holding meetings here, telling about a powerful 'Creator-God' that is a kind God. Would you come to our village and tell us about Him?"

Adolphe watched her. She was dressed in a pink-flowered *lamba* and looked down at her hands while she spoke. Her voice was sincere and pleading. He thought for a while, and then he answered. "Yes, we will try to come tomorrow afternoon. But first I must talk to the others." Kalovary looked up, smiled, and then hurried away without another word.

Adolphe turned back to the table where he had been praying, and he thought how similar she was to the shy, young woman he used to teach in Ampanihy (ump-ah-NEE-hee). But as a young Malagasy teacher, he had felt the call to full-time service and had left his promising teaching career to become a pastor.

Ninety years earlier, Lutheran missionaries had brought the light of the Gospel to this island nation off the southeast coast of Africa. Congregations were started. Bible schools and seminaries were established. National pastors and workers were trained to go with the missionaries into remote villages and preach the Word of God. Adolphe, especially, had a gift of ministering to people and had been discipled for several years by the missionaries.

After his ordination, Adolphe worked mainly in Ampanihy with several young catechists (Bible school graduates) bringing the Gospel to the surrounding villages. At the time, they were holding three-day meetings in Votovoatavo. Three-day meetings like these were held every three months around the district.

Later that afternoon, Adolphe, together with the missionary and the catechists, gathered for prayer. As they knelt, they knew tomorrow would be difficult—impossible if they were to rely on their own power. For Behera was a village where the Gospel had never been preached. Here the forces of darkness had been in control for centuries.

The people of Behera were enslaved by their traditional, animistic religions. They had built shrines or altars to various spirits and, in some cases, to the ancestors. At these altars, villagers prayed and offered sacrifices to appease the spirits. Sometimes the shrines were rocks, sometimes strange looking trees, but always the Malagasy people believed that the spirits living within these objects held power over them. In fact, they believed these spirits were so powerful that if one approached an altar without correct sacrifices, snakes, lightening, or other evil forces would destroy the person.

Knowing the difficulties they were to face, the Christians prayed for power over the evil one and for God to govern their every word.

The next day in Behera, they gathered in the shade of some Kily (KEE-lee) trees. The hot sun blazed brightly on the dry, dusty village in the desert-like region of south central Madagascar.

The tall missionary placed his autoharp on the hood of the cream-colored panel truck and began singing:

> The love of God is greater far
> Than tongue or pen can ever tell;
> It goes beyond the highest star
> And reaches to the lowest hell.

Attracted by this strange, light-skinned *vazaha*, the villagers gathered around listening to song after song. The Malagasy people have beautiful singing voices and love to sing, but this was something different. They had never heard songs like this before.

When the songs ended, the missionary put away his harp, and he and Adolphe began preaching about the love of the "Creator-God" that had sent His Son to die for the people of Behera.

Suddenly, from the back of the crowd, a man named Reholahiny (ray-hah-lah-HEE-nee) jumped up and shouted: "Stop telling lies! You have your Jesus, but I have this Kily tree." He pointed to a lush, green Kily tree a short distance away. "I receive my children, cattle, sheep, goats, and everything I need for life from that tree. Get out of here. We won't stand for your silly storytelling."

Andre, one of the catechists, stood up and said, "No, it is Jesus, the One we are telling you about today, who gives you all you need. He also gives true happiness."

Reholahiny became furious and stomped his foot on the ground: "Get out of our village at once. Let us live as our fathers lived. Leave us to the wrath of God. Leave us alone."

"We won't argue and fight with you," Adolphe replied. "According to the Bible, the book I'm holding in my hand, vengeance belongs to God. He will do what is best for you." With that, the small band of Christians ended their meeting and returned to Votovoatavo.

The next day while he was praying, Adolphe again heard someone coughing outside the door. But today it was more frantic. When he opened the door, he saw Kalovary again. This time she was smiling. "Yesterday, after you had gone home, my brother Reholahiny said to me, 'Tonight you will die! It was you who brought those praying people here to disturb our peace. The gods don't like that, and tonight you will die!'"

"But see," she said, holding her arms wide apart, "nothing happened to me during the night, and here I am as well as I have ever been." And then with such excitement she could hardly control herself, she exclaimed, "You must come back to Behera with me. Something amazing has happened!"

So they all returned to Behera. Kalovary led them through the village to the Kily tree that Reholahiny had told them was the god he worshiped. There before their eyes stood a dead tree. What had been a lush, green tree yesterday had mysteriously withered and died overnight. All that was

Jack Ringdahl, age 6

left were bare branches and a bare trunk. Beneath it a pile of leaves lay, shriveled and yellow.

Gathered around the tree, villagers stood muttering, trying to explain what had happened. No one had an answer, except Kalovary. "This is God's doing," she exclaimed. "He has more power than my brother's tree. Now I want to follow this God. Teach me His ways, so I can be baptized and become a Christian."

And thus it was in April of 1954 in the village of Behara, God showed His miraculous power, and the light of the Gospel finally penetrated the darkness that had covered this village for centuries.

QUESTIONS:
1. Why did it seem difficult to Adolphe and the others to bring the Gospel to the village of Behera?
2. What kind of power did Reholahiny think his Kily tree had?
3. Why didn't Kalovary die as her brother predicted?
4. Explain what happened to the Kily tree and the village of Behara.

Amos Dyrud graduated from Augsburg Seminary in 1949. Upon graduation, Amos and Ovidie left for Madagascar where they served as missionaries from 1949-1969, first under the Lutheran Free Church and later under the American Lutheran Church. Upon returning to the United States, Pastor Dyrud began teaching at AFLTS and AFLBS and served as Dean of Association Free Lutheran Theological Seminary from 1971-1981. For several years thereafter, he was a part-time instructor at AFLTS and AFLBS. He and Ovidie are retired and live in Crystal, Minnesota, where they are members of Grace Free Lutheran Church in Maple Grove. Amos is the "missionary" in this story. (For further reading about missionary life in Madagascar, see Each for the Other: All for Christ, *a biography of the Dyruds available from Ambassador Publications.)*

"Almost Persuaded"

By Amos O. Dyrud
(as told to Loiell Dyrud)

On the edge of Ampanihy (ump-ah-NEE-hee), a village in southwestern Madagascar, there lived an *ombiasa* (OOM-bee-AH-shah) or witch doctor. His name was Ebolasy (eh-boh-LAH-shee), and he was one of the richest and most powerful men in the village. For months, Adolphe Santinely (SAHNT-ah-NEL-ee), the young Malagasy evangelist, had been burdened for the soul of Ebolasy. He spent hours praying for him and witnessed to him every chance he had.

Since Adolphe had lived his entire life in Ampanihy, he had seen many of the witch doctor's evil acts. He had seen how he held people under his power, how he worked his charms predicting futures, casting spells, and warding off evil spirits. No matter what the *ombiasa* predicted, most people believed in him and paid him anything he asked. If they had no money, they paid him in chickens, cattle, or goats.

This morning as he walked up the path to Ebolasy's hut, Adolphe saw him working on a charm. He was sitting on a small mat of woven hemp, spread carefully on the sand. On top of the mat, he had placed several kernels of corn, arranging them in patterns and muttering over them. He was working out a *sikidy* (sah-KEE-dee), or magical charm.

Adolphe watched him sadly. He thought of how much evil the *ombiasas* performed through the power of Satan. How years earlier, the French government had banned their worst practice—killing babies shortly after they were born. Even though it had been outlawed for more than fifty years, the government still had not been able to eliminate the practice completely. Not too far from their own village, Adolphe had heard, infanticide was still being practiced.

When a baby was born, the witch doctor, through his *sikidy*, would decide whether the child should live or die. If born on an unlucky day, the child would be put to death or the village would be cursed. Often parents were told their dead ancestors would come back to haunt the village if they did not obey. Sometimes the baby was buried alive, sometimes crushed with heavy rocks, sometimes trampled by stampeding cattle, and sometimes placed on top of a giant anthill to be eaten alive by the ants. But all the time, the witch doctor had the final say, and no amount of parental pleading made any difference.

The *ombiasa* also controlled the villagers' daily lives. Non-Christians went to him for advice on almost everything—how to treat illness, how to increase fertility of their cattle, or how to rid evil spirits. And always, the witch doctor demanded a healthy payment.

After Adolphe had finished training at the Lutheran Bible School and been called as an evangelist, he had grieved over the villagers trapped by the witch doctor's spell. If only Ebolasy would give his heart to the Lord, he reasoned, how much suffering could be removed from this village. So for months, he had been witnessing to him.

At first Ebolasy flew into a rage when Adolphe mentioned Christ, but recently he seemed more restrained. Often he would sit cross-legged on the sand, deep in thought, while Adolphe talked to him about Jesus, the Son of the Creator-God.

The church in Ampanihy was finally completed. For years the missionaries and the Malagasy had worked on this building. Now at last, the steeple rose into the sky, high above every other building, announcing to all the presence of God in the village. Even the interior sparkled with a fresh coat of whitewash.

This afternoon would mark the first series of evangelistic meetings in the new church, and Adolphe would be speaking.

"Ebolasy," Adolphe started the conversation, "Ebolasy, the Christ I worship loves you and wants to give you peace. Why not come to our church and hear more about Him?"

Ebolasy stared at his charms and didn't say a word. This was not the first time Adolphe had asked him to come to church. But these last few visits, Ebolasy was at least listening and not cursing under his breath. Adolphe sensed the Holy Spirit was working on him.

Today as Adolphe spoke, Ebolasy kept tapping his finger on the cattle horn tied around his waist. In the doorway, Ebolasy's wife stood watching their two sons playing in the sand. She, too, was listening. Through Adolphe's encouragement, the boys had begun coming to Sunday School. And during the recent visits, she had been coming to the doorway, listening intently to every word Adolphe spoke.

"Ebolasy, I will be speaking about the love of Jesus this afternoon. Why don't you come to the church and hear more about this Jesus?"

There was a long pause. Ebolasy shook his head. Adolphe invited him again. "Why not come and bring the family? We have appreciated having your fine-looking, young boys in our Sunday School these last two Sundays."

This time Ebolasy looked up, "Maybe. Maybe I will come this afternoon."

"Please, do," Adolphe said. "I'll be watching for you."

As Adolphe walked back to the village, he prayed, "O Jesus, let Your Holy Spirit work a miracle in Ebolasy's heart. Help me say the words You want me to say. Lord, let him see his lost condition and repent." That day, as the missionaries and Malagasy Christians prayed for the service, they prayed especially for Ebolasy.

Late that afternoon, the service began. The Malagasy sang song after song, but no sign of Ebolasy. Finally, as the song before the sermon was sung, Ebolasy, his wife, and their two boys walked into the church. He was not wearing his charms. The horns and bones and beads were left behind.

Adolphe rejoiced as the Malagasy sang:

> Softly and tenderly Jesus is calling,
> Calling for you and for me;
> See, on the portals He's waiting and watching,
> Watching for you and for me.
> Come home, come home,
> You who are weary come home;
> Earnestly, tenderly, Jesus is calling—
> Calling, "O sinner, come home!"

That night Adolphe spoke as he had never spoken before. He told about the Creator-God's Son, Jesus, who loved us so much He came down from His palace in heaven to live with us on earth. He explained how our evil ways had led to His death on the cross so that we would not have to die.

While Adolphe preached and the missionaries prayed, Ebolasy sat on the bench deep in thought. At times he looked down, but most of the time his eyes were locked on Adolphe, and he seemed to drink in every word. But his wife sat motionless, stone-faced, staring straight ahead.

When Adolphe was almost to the end of his sermon, Ebolasy's wife bent over to him, pulled on his arm, and whispered in his ear. Adolphe

Andrew Quanbeck, age 14

watched Ebolasy's face slowly change. A stern look came over him, and he got up and walked out into the dying light. His wife and sons followed in single file.

The next morning, Adolphe walked to Ebolasy's hut. He was sitting on the ground in the hot sun. In front of him, his mat displayed a careful arrangement of charms. Around his neck hung two cow horns and a goat horn packed with magical potions. Tufts of twisted, black hair, animal teeth, small bones, and red, white, and black beads were hanging from his chest. He was fitfully working on a *sikidy*.

"Ebolasy, why did you walk out while I was speaking yesterday? What did your wife say to you?"

Ebolasy looked up. His eyes were cold and black, and he stared straight at Adolphe. "She asked me what we would do if I become a Christian? She asked me how we would live if I quit being an *ombiasa*? She said it would be awful to live in poverty. 'It wouldn't be fair for our boys. And what would our ancestors think?' No, Adolphe, I've decided this is my life. I want to live in the traditions of my ancestors. I don't want to hear any more about your Jesus. Don't come back!" In the doorway, Ebolasy's wife stood triumphantly, arms across her chest.

Adolphe turned. He had taken only a few steps when Ebolasy called, "And one more thing, Adolphe. My charms are stronger than your Jesus. One of these days to prove it, I'm going to call down lightning on your new church. I'll strike the steeple and burn it to the ground. Then we'll see whose god is stronger!" Adolphe walked back to the village, his head bowed in disappointment.

Lightning never did strike the church in Ampanihy, his boys never returned to Sunday School, and Ebolasy never set foot inside the sanctuary again. He had hardened his heart. But within a year, both his sons had died. Not one of his charms had the power to save them.

QUESTIONS:
1. Not all missionary stories are success stories. From what you have discovered while reading this story, comment on some of the difficulties missionaries experience trying to reach people in foreign lands?
2. The title of the story is taken from this song:
    "Almost persuaded" Now to believe;
    "Almost persuaded" Christ to receive;

> Seems now some soul to say, "Go Spirit, go Thy way,
> Some more convenient day on Thee I'll call."

How does this song contribute to the meaning of the story?
3. Who is responsible for Ebolasy rejecting Christ?

Amos Dyrud graduated from Augsburg Seminary in 1949. Upon graduation, Amos and Ovidie left for Madagascar where they served as missionaries from 1949-1969, first under the Lutheran Free Church and later under the American Lutheran Church. Upon returning to the United States, Pastor Dyrud began teaching at AFLTS and AFLBS and served as Dean of Association Free Lutheran Theological Seminary from 1971-1981. For several years thereafter, he was a part-time instructor at AFLTS and AFLBS. He and Ovidie are retired and live in Crystal, Minnesota, where they are members of Grace Free Lutheran Church in Maple Grove. (For further reading about missionary life in Madagascar, see Each for the Other: All for Christ, *a biography of the Dyruds available from Ambassador Publications.)*

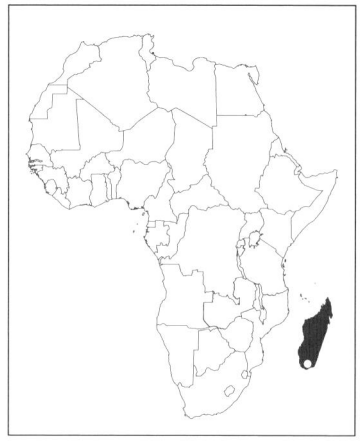

A Bell Rings for Koroline

By Amos O. Dyrud

In the early 1950s, a large stone church in the center of Ampanihy (ump-ah-NEE-hee), Madagascar, was being built. Since all the work was done by hand, many local bricklayers and carpenters had to be hired along with many common laborers who assisted in any way they could. Tons of cement and sand were mixed into mortar with shovels, spades, and buckets of water. Then the mortar was hoisted thirty feet up to the top of the wall with block and tackle.

Because so many workers were needed, they had to look beyond Ampanihy for help. Efoterana (eh-foh-tay-RAH-nah) had come from a neighboring village and proved to be a good worker—serious and faithful.

As was the custom in Madagascar, everyone settled down after lunch for a rest under the trees to get away from the hot, glaring sun. This proved to be the perfect time for Pastor Adolphe Santinely (SAHNT-ah-NEL-ee), a Malagasy evangelist, to give "learning-to-read" lessons. He often included the Bible as one of his texts. Efoterana and his wife, Koroline (kohr-oh-LEEN), were eager to take part in this study. Missionaries Pastor Amos Dyrud and his wife, Ovidie, had prayed that the Bible reading would catch the interest of those studying with Pastor Santinely. It seemed to be happening, for some of the workers began attending the church service.

After a few weeks, Pastor Dyrud asked Pastor Santinely how his classes were going. "Oh," he said sadly, "it has gone well for a while, but now Koroline has quit studying. It looks as if she has found other interests."

Refusing to be discouraged, neither Santinely nor the missionaries stopped praying for her. They knew that the Lord wanted her to come to know Him as her personal Savior. They also knew that she had heard God's Word in Pastor Santinely's Bible classes, and God had promised in Isaiah 55:11 that His Word would accomplish what He desired.

A few days after talking with Pastor Santinely, Pastor Dyrud and Ovidie began hearing loud noises, drums beating in the countryside near Ampanihy. Night after night it continued. One evening, curious to find the source, Pastor Dyrud began walking toward the insistent din of the drums. From a distance, he could see a crowd of people gathered in a circle, some sitting, some standing. When he got closer, he saw an *ombiasa* (OOM-bee-AH-shah), a witch doctor, together with drummers and dancers, carrying out the heathen ritual of casting out the evil spirit of sickness from the person sitting in the center of the circle.

"Oh, no!" Pastor Dyrud exclaimed. To his great sorrow, he recognized the woman in the center. It was Efoterana's wife, Koroline, looking disheveled, lonely, and sick.

When they saw the missionary, the drummers stopped. The dancers stopped. Efoterana walked up to the missionary and then looked away in embarrassment. "What has happened? Why are you doing this?" Pastor Dyrud asked.

"Koroline is so sick," he replied. "We thought the witch doctor and the drumming and dancing would help. That's why we tried this ritual. We wanted to see if she would get well."

Pastor Dyrud left and walked sadly home. He gathered his family together to pray that the power of God would set Efoterana and Koroline free from the heathen darkness and gloom.

Early the next morning, there was a loud knock on the Dyruds' door. It was Efoterana. "Please, come right away and baptize Koroline," he said in a trembling voice.

As Pastor Dyrud entered their house, he saw Koroline lying on the floor, clutching a pillow and writhing in pain. "Do you need Jesus the Savior now?" asked Pastor Dyrud.

"Yes," was her firm reply.

"Do you want to be baptized?" he asked.

And again she answered, "Yes."

By then Pastor Santinely had arrived. Together the pastors shared Scripture and prayed. Koroline was baptized. Then the three men took her to the hospital.

Fortunately, Dr. Kalsef, an itinerant medical doctor, was there. After he examined her, he said, "She should have had medical help long ago. Her heart is seriously sick."

The two pastors visited Koroline every day. One day they found she had been moved to a small, private room. As they walked in, the atmosphere seemed heavenly. God was so near! Pastor Santinely read from

Lydia Ackerman, age 6

John 14:1-3: "Do not let your heart be troubled; believe in God, believe also in me. In my Father's house are many dwelling places; if it were not so, I would have told you; for I go to prepare a place for you. If I go and prepare a place for you, I will come again and receive you to Myself, that where I am, there you may be also." Pastor Dyrud prayed that God's will would be done, that Jesus would be glorified.

Early the next morning, the bell in the church steeple was ringing. It is a Malagasy custom to ring the bell when a believer in Christ dies.

Pastor Dyrud and Ovidie looked at each other and asked, "Do you suppose the bell is ringing for Koroline?" It was true. She had died during the night. In His loving kindness and tender mercy, Jesus had taken Koroline's soul home to heaven.

QUESTIONS:
1. What did Pastor Dyrud discover when he walked toward the sound of the drums?
2. Why did Efoterana come to the missionary and anxiously ask him to come and baptize his wife?
3. What does the word "believe" mean?
4. What does Jesus promise to all who believe in Him? (John 14:1-3)

Amos Dyrud graduated from Augsburg Seminary in 1949. Upon graduation, Amos and Ovidie left for Madagascar where they served as missionaries from 1949-1969, first under the Lutheran Free Church and later under the American Lutheran Church. Upon returning to the United States, Pastor Dyrud began teaching at AFLTS and AFLBS and served as Dean of Association Free Lutheran Theological Seminary from 1971-1981. For several years thereafter, he was a part-time instructor at AFLTS and AFLBS. He and Ovidie are retired and live in Crystal, Minnesota, where they are members of Grace Free Lutheran Church in Maple Grove. (For further reading about missionary life in Madagascar, see Each for the Other: All for Christ*, a biography of the Dyruds available from Ambassador Publications.)*

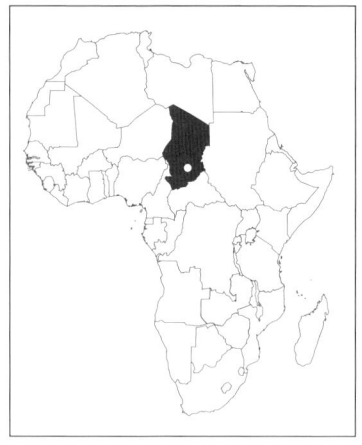

More Powerful Than Satan

By Rachel Chesley

Bill had known Moussa (MOO-sah) for many years. He was a faithful Muslim, who always stopped his work when it was time for the daily prayers. Moussa had supervised all the masonry work on their house when the Chesley family first moved to Baro (BAH-roh), in Chad, Africa. But now Moussa approached Bill with a look of deep concern on his lined and weather-beaten face. His long robe swished faintly as he walked. A turban protected his eyes from the hot sun and dust.

"My wife is very ill," he said. "Would you please take me to Mongo (MONG-oh) so I can bring her back home? I took her to the doctors at the hospital, but they could not help her. Then I took her to the imam (EE-mom), the Muslim teacher, but his prayers could not help her either. Now I just want to bring her home."

"What is wrong with your wife?" Bill asked.

"Satan has made my wife ill," Moussa replied.

A trip to Mongo would be long and expensive, so Bill thought of another way he could help Moussa. He gave Moussa some money so that he could travel on a market truck to Mongo and then purchase two seats for the return trip. Moussa was very grateful.

Before Moussa left, Bill said, "Jesus the Messiah is stronger than Satan. If Satan has made your wife ill, Jesus can help her. When you bring her home, I will come and pray for you if you like."

Bill knew that the Migaama (mee-GAH-mah) people lived in fear of the powers of darkness. But Bill also knew that Jesus had defeated the powers of darkness through His death as stated in Colossians 2:15: "When He had disarmed the rulers and authorities, He made a public dis-

Andrew Horn, age 16

play of them, having triumphed over them through Him."

Moussa left and was gone for several days. Bill had nearly forgotten about Moussa and his promise to pray. But then one day, Moussa came again and said, "My wife is at home now. You promised that you would come and pray for her."

As they hurried along to Moussa's house under the hot sun, Bill asked again about his wife's illness.

"She has terrible tremors," Moussa said. "Her hands shake so badly that she cannot do anything. She cannot cook, she cannot sweep the house, she cannot even make tea."

When they arrived at Moussa's house, Bill was shown to a straw mat in a shaded area. Moussa's wife, Hawa (HAH-wah), came and sat nearby. She was a small woman, dressed in a flowing *lafay* (lah-FIE), which covered all but her face and hands. Her eyes were downcast. She did not greet Bill or speak at all.

Bill began to pray, "Father, we do not know from where this sickness has come. But we know that You are stronger than Satan, for You defeated Satan on the cross of Christ. You can make this woman well if You desire. If Satan has brought this illness upon Hawa, we ask You to free her from Satan's power. Please take away her tremors and restore her health. We ask You in Jesus' name, the name that is above every name. Amen."

Moussa served Bill a tiny glass full of strong, sweet tea. As he returned home, Bill prayed silently that God would make Hawa well and bring faith to this Muslim family.

Several days passed before Moussa came again to Bill's house. When he arrived, there was a glad light in his eyes. "My wife is healed!" he said. "Jesus has made my wife well. She has no more tremors. She can cook and work around the house." God had answered Bill's prayer, even as He promised in Mark 11:24: "Therefore I say to you, all things for which you pray and ask, believe that you have received them, and they will be granted you."

Moussa became more serious as he added, "The doctors in Mongo could not heal my wife. Even the imam and his prayers could not heal my wife. But Jesus the Messiah has healed my wife. From now on, I will follow Jesus. I no longer recite the Muslim prayers. I will come to church now."

True to his word, Moussa has continued to attend church and follow Jesus the Messiah.

QUESTIONS:
1. What two kinds of healing took place in this story?
2. Which was more important and why?
3. Who healed Hawa?
4. Do you believe that God always answers your prayers?

Rachel (Mundfrom) Chesley was raised in North and South Dakota, the daughter of Rev. and Mrs. Gerald Mundfrom. She graduated from AFLBS in 1978 and from the University of Arizona in 1981 with a degree in Speech and Language Disorders. She also studied linguistics at the University of North Dakota and the University of Texas. In 1989 she joined Wycliffe Bible Translators and has been serving with her husband, Bill, in Chad, Africa, since 1990. They started a Bible translation and literacy work among the Migaama people of central Chad in 1996.

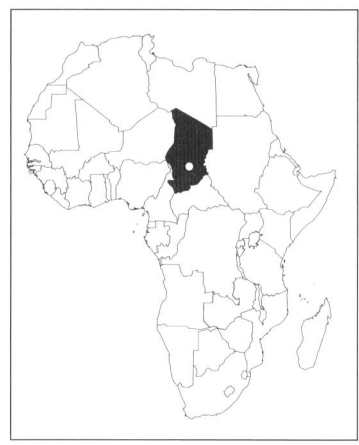

Bernincha's Bracelet

By Rachel Chesley

Bernincha (bur-NIHN-chah) laughed as her brothers chased her through the tall stalks of ripening millet outside their home in central Chad, Africa. They would catch up to her soon, she knew, but it was all in fun. Bernincha was so glad that she was three years old now—old enough to play with her brothers and older sister. Her baby sister never got to run around and never got to play at the house of the missionaries, Bill and Rachel Chesley.

The Chesley children had lots of toys. Often on Sundays after church, Bichara, Ouda, Marie, and Bernincha would go to the Chesley house to play with Emily, Lydia, and David and have lunch together. Bernincha's favorite toys were the tiny cars and trucks with real tires that you could push along on the floor. Bernincha had not ridden in a car or truck very often. But her papa had a motorcycle, and she often rode on that. She was not afraid like some other children.

Bernincha looked down at her wrist and fingered the colorful beads on the bracelet she wore. Her papa was the pastor of the church, and her parents had received many of these bracelets to give out at church. Bernincha could still remember very clearly the message this bracelet, with all its colors, was meant to teach.

Her teacher had held up the bracelet and pointed to the yellow bead, "This bead stands for heaven. Jesus said, 'I go to prepare a place for you' (John 14:2). Who is heaven being prepared for?"

"All the Christians," was the children's response.

"You know what?" the teacher replied, "Jesus would like everyone to go to heaven. But will everyone get there?"

"No," said a little boy in the front.

The teacher pointed to the black bead. "This bead stands for our sin. Isaiah 59:2 says that our sins have hidden God's face from us so that He does not hear our prayers."

Bernincha listened intently. She knew this was true. When we disobey, our sins separate us from God.

Now the teacher pointed to the red bead. "Who can tell me what this bead stands for? What can take away our sin?"

Bethany Berntson, age 12

Bernincha knew the answer. "Jesus' blood!" she called out.

"That's right. The blood of Jesus cleanses us from all sin (I John 1:7). And when God has made us clean, our hearts are no longer black like this bead. Instead, they are like this white one, just as white as cotton. How many of you have hearts that have been made white by Jesus' blood?"

Many hands went up. The teacher gave bracelets to everyone, telling them to be sure to tell the story of the colored beads to their parents and to friends who were not coming to Sunday School.

When Bernincha got home, she asked, "Can I please have five bracelets, Papa? I want two for my wrists, two for my ankles, and one for my neck!"

"No, no, little one. You must be satisfied with just one," answered Papa.

But Bernincha soon found a way to get more bracelets. Her brothers were not careful with theirs. In fact, they didn't want to wear them all the time. After a few weeks, their bracelets were all but forgotten. Bernincha noticed when the bracelets were discarded thoughtlessly and ran to pick them up. Because of this, she was often able to wear at least a bracelet and necklace and sometimes even two bracelets and a necklace.

One day Papa had an announcement for all the family to hear. "We are going to go on a long journey," he said. "There is a school for Christian workers where I will study for one year, and all of you will go with me."

It was early September, and the rains were still heavy. Someone else would have to harvest the millet and the sesame and the peanuts. It seemed very strange to be leaving. This village was the only home Bernincha had known.

The trip was very long, and the roads were muddy. But finally they arrived at the place that would be their home for the next year. As Mother got them settled in this new place, Bernincha followed her brothers and sister in getting to know the other children and finding new games to play. She wouldn't be sad for long, even though she missed her home back in the village.

One day not long after their arrival, Bernincha put down her playthings and went to find her mother. "My head hurts, Mommy," she said.

Her mother gathered her close to comfort her. She felt the feverish body and knew that Bernincha was very sick. She hoped that a lukewarm bath would help to bring the fever down, but later in the day there was no improvement. Bernincha's mother placed cool cloths on her little body and went to find her husband.

"What can we do for Bernincha? Should we take her to the clinic?"

"It is too late to go to the clinic today," he said. "We will pray for Bernincha tonight, and if she is not better in the morning, I will take her."

The family gathered around Bernincha and prayed for her. Then they tucked her into bed.

In the morning her little body was still very hot. Her aching head made her cry out in pain. Her father knew that she needed medicine and prepared to take her to the clinic. It was not far away, and he could easily carry his small daughter. He began to remove the bracelets from Bernincha's neck and wrist, but she roused enough to protest.

"No, Papa! I want to keep them on!"

The people at the clinic were kind and helpful, but the medicine they gave Bernincha was too late to help. The malaria had attacked her body with too much force, and she died later that day. To the very end, she insisted on wearing her bracelets, a symbol of her hope and faith.

QUESTIONS:
1. Why did Bernincha like the bracelets so much?
2. What would be a good name for a bracelet with beads like these? Why?
3. What happened to Bernincha when she died?

Rachel (Mundfrom) Chesley was raised in North and South Dakota, the daughter of Rev. and Mrs. Gerald Mundfrom. She graduated from AFLBS in 1978 and from the University of Arizona in 1981 with a degree in Speech and Language Disorders. She also studied linguistics at the University of North Dakota and the University of Texas. In 1989 she joined Wycliffe Bible Translators and has been serving with her husband, Bill, in Chad, Africa, since 1990. They started a Bible translation and literacy work among the Migaama people of central Chad in 1996.

Tabletop Appendectomy

By Jerry and Maija Carlson

Jerry and Maija (MY-ah) Carlson worked on the Makki (MAH-kee) mission station in a remote area of southwest Ethiopia. The closest mission station to them was a five-hour journey over difficult roads. Jinka (JIN-kah), the nearest town to their mission station, was forty-three miles away. To get to Jinka, one had to ford the Makki River and travel twelve miles along a dirt trail that was almost overgrown with thorn bushes. The next twelve miles were through more open, thorn bush country. In these first twenty-four miles of the trip, there were lions, elephants, buffalo, and other wild animals to watch out for. Besides the wild animals, there were the tsetse (TSET-see) flies to contend with—flying insects about the size of a horse fly. The bite of this fly feels like being touched with a red-hot iron. In many parts of Africa, the tsetse fly carries the dreaded "sleeping sickness." Jerry and Maija always prayed that they would not have to get out and change a flat tire in the tsetse fly area! After getting through this area, there were still nineteen more miles of very narrow mountain roads before reaching the destination of Jinka.

Jerry and Maija drove a 4-wheel-drive Toyota equipped with a winch to travel these rough, treacherous, and often muddy roads. Wherever they drove, their journeys would start with praying to the Lord for safety. They always carried two spare tires, tools and patches to repair flat tires, a tire pump, a shovel, two sets of tire chains, two jacks, and some short pieces of heavy boards to set the jacks on. In the dry season, it usually took at least three hours to drive the forty-three miles to Jinka, depending on how muddy the road was and how many flat tires they got from thorns along the way.

One day in the rainy season, Jerry said to Maija, "I'm having really bad pains in the lower right side of my body. Do you think it is from the goat meat we ate yesterday?" Maija, being a nurse, did some checking and probing and found that the pain was sharper when she removed her finger from the tender area than when she pressed on it.

"Jerry," Maija said, "I think it is your appendix that is causing the pain. You will have to get to a hospital where you may need to have your appendix removed. If it should rupture, it could be fatal."

The nearest hospital was at Arba Minch, another eight hours beyond Jinka. It was the rainy season, though, and the roads would be rough, muddy, and possibly impassable in places. With appendicitis, it would be an unbearable trip. The one thing Jerry and Maija could do was turn to the Lord in prayer.

"Lord, we turn to you in this time of desperate need," Jerry prayed. "You brought us here to bring the Good News to the Mursi (MUR-see) people, and we know that You will meet all our needs. I am in need of medical attention, and I cannot make the trip by car to the hospital. We pray that You will intercede in this situation. May Your will be done. Thank You, Lord."

Each mission station has radio communication with the SIM headquarters in Addis Ababa (AD-dis ah-BAY-bah) twice a day, at 8 A.M. and 6 P.M. When the 6 P.M. radio time came around, Maija told mission headquarters, "Jerry is having an appendicitis problem. He needs to get to a hospital for a possible operation. I think the roads are almost impassable. Jerry will not be able to endure the rough, long trip even if we could get through. Are you able to help us?"

It is amazing how the Lord often has things worked out even before we call on Him. In Ethiopia at that time, there was a Swiss mission agency called Helimission that provided helicopter service for mission work. Also at this time, there was a highly skilled Australian surgeon at mission headquarters in Addis Ababa! When Jerry and Maija had not been on their radio for two radio schedules in a row, the mission director at the SIM headquarters was concerned that their station might have had a visit from armed bandits since two of the neighboring mission stations had recently had problems with bandits. The mission director had already made arrangements to send someone down in a helicopter to check on the Makki mission station.

The Lord had all things prepared ahead of time: a helicopter, a doctor, and a plan for a flight to check on Jerry and Maija! The next morning as soon as the helicopter could leave Addis Ababa, the doctor and an extra nurse headed to the remote Makki mission station in southwest Ethiopia and landed in the Carlson's front yard. After a few preparations, the doctor gave Jerry a spinal anesthetic and then had him lie down on the dining room table. The Mursi friends stood outside, pressing their noses against the window to see what was happening to "Mr. Jerry."

Erin Schram, age 17

The group inside the house paused to pray for the Lord's help: "Our Father, this is a difficult time for Jerry and Maija. Please help us to do this surgery in the very best way. We acknowledge You to be our healer of all ills and thank You for Your presence with us. Amen." With two nurses assisting and the helicopter pilot shining a flashlight on the operation site, the skilled hands of the doctor removed the troubling appendix.

Within an hour and a half from the time the doctor and nurse arrived at the Makki station, they were again on their way back to Addis Ababa, and Jerry was on his way to a speedy recovery. The Lord does hear and answer prayers even before we ask Him. Jerry and Maija remembered God's promise in Isaiah 65:24: "It will also come to pass that before they call, I will answer; and while they are still speaking, I will hear."

QUESTIONS:
1. What happened to Jerry?
2. How did God provide for Jerry and Maija?
3. How can you help missionaries serving in isolated areas of the world?
4. Can you think of situations where God has already had the answer to your prayer on the way even before you prayed?

Jerry first went to Tanzania, Africa, as an agricultural missionary in 1962 under the Lutheran Free Church. There he met and married Maija Neuvonen, a missionary nurse/midwife from Finland. Later they served as missionaries in Ethiopia under the American Lutheran Church and as houseparents for missionary children in Cameroon under the Lutheran Brethren Church. After some time in the U.S., they felt called to return to Africa where they began a new outreach to the Mursi people under Sudan Interior Mission (SIM). They are presently retired and living in McVille, North Dakota, where they are members of New Luther Valley Lutheran Church. They have on occasion returned to Ethiopia for short-term mission work.

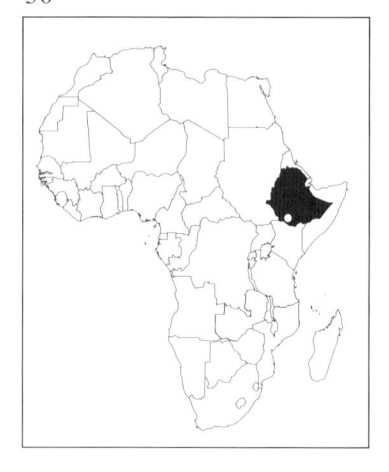

Eagle Wings to the Rescue

By Jerry and Maija Carlson

It was a clear, bright morning as missionaries Jerry and Maija (MY-ah) loaded their 4-wheel-drive vehicle with medicine and headed out on "mobile clinic" to a remote area of Mursi (MUR-see) country in southwest Ethiopia where the Mursi people graze their cattle. The Mursi people are called nomads because they usually don't live permanently in one place. Cattle are their bank account—the most important resource in their lives. And they are constantly on the move in order to find grass and water for their cattle. Often the Mursi men, women, and children out in the grazing area are in need of medical help but can't leave their cattle and walk the long distance to the clinic at the Makki (MAH-kee) mission station. With the mobile clinic, Maija and Jerry can provide medical help and also take the opportunity to introduce the nomadic Mursi to God's Word.

"It's time to head out to Mursi country to see if anyone has any medical needs," Jerry told Maija. "Looks like you've packed some other supplies too."

"Yes," she responded, "besides the medical supplies, I've packed the Gospel Recording picture book, the tape recorder, and some other tapes telling the story of Jesus so we can share the Gospel with them also. As usual, we will also take Evangelist Abraham along with us."

Recently the Bodi (BOH-dee) people, a neighboring tribe to the Mursi, had made a raid on one of the Mursi cattle camps and had gotten away with some of the Mursi's cattle. Jerry and Maija were not aware of this new conflict. Otherwise they would not have gone on mobile clinic work that day. But the Lord knew of the conflict, and He knew that someone was in desperate need of medical help. He also knew that there were many Mursi who needed to hear about Jesus and how He could change their lives.

Jerry and Maija had to ford the Makki River that is near the Makki mission station. This day the water in the river only came up to the running boards on their vehicle as they drove across. In the rainy season, it can be so deep that it would come over the car's hood. After crossing the river, there were many miles yet to drive on a rough, rutted, and stony track that was almost overgrown with brush. The second river, the Mago (MAH-goh) River, had a bridge over it, so there was no difficulty in getting across. After crossing the Mago River Bridge, the next part of the trip was to climb a rocky road that wound up the edge of steep cliffs on some very high hills.

"I'm glad it's the dry season, so we don't have to contend with washed out areas on the road," said Maija. "That would make the drive impossible!"

When they reached the top, there were still many miles of stony, dirt roads to go.

"Hang on," laughed Jerry as they jostled and bumped over the rough

Morgan Mairs, age 13

road. "We've gone about as far as we can on this road. Now we'll have to drive through the thorn bush country to look for the Mursi camp."

It took longer than usual to find the Mursi cattle camp because the people were trying to hide themselves and their cattle from their enemies. Jerry and Maija knew that the cattle camp would be in an enclosure made of thorn bushes built by the Mursi people to keep their cattle in during the night to protect them from lions and hyenas. There would also be a few temporary huts for the men and their families to sleep in.

Finally, they spotted the camp. As they arrived, the people came running and shouting in their native language, "Maija, come quickly and help the man in this hut!" The Mursi hut is a grass, igloo-shaped hut about ten feet in diameter and eight feet high with a door so low you have to get on your hands and knees to enter it. Because there are no windows, it is quite dark on the inside. When Maija crawled into the hut and got her eyes adjusted to the dim light, she found Logolanyhulu (LOH-goh-lah-nee-HOO-loo), a Mursi friend of theirs who had often helped as translator on mobile clinics.

Maija asked, "Logolanyhulu, what has happened to you?"

Greeting Maija, Logolanyhulu exclaimed, "Oh, Nurse Maija! How are you? I am so glad to see you! I have a very big problem. When the Bodi made their raid on us, I was shot in the wrist and ankle. I managed to escape and have been lying here for five days, waiting and hoping that help would come."

Maija spent over an hour picking the maggots out of the wounds and disinfecting and putting dressings on them. "We will need to get you to the hospital so you can be treated properly to heal," she said. It was obvious that he needed medical treatment at a hospital if his hand and foot were to be saved.

While Maija was taking care of Logolanyhulu, Evangelist Abraham and Jerry were showing the Gospel Recording picture book and playing the accompanying tape for the other Mursi who were gathered around.

After Maija treated some other patients, Jerry and Maija and Abraham took Logolanyhulu, his wife, and small child back to the mission station. They had to hurry in order to get back in time for the 6:00 evening radio schedule. Jerry requested that Missionary Aviation Fellowship (MAF) send a plane to pick up Logolanyhulu and take him to the mission hospital in Arba Minch. It would take ten hours by road, traveling through mountains and desert, but it would only take thirty minutes by plane.

That night Maija and Jerry prayed, "Dear Father, please have a plane available for this mission, and grant that the weather will allow the flight to get our friend Logolanyhulu to the hospital for treatment. Thank You, in Jesus' name. Amen."

The Lord was gracious and answered their prayer. Like an eagle soaring in the sky, a plane came early the next morning and took the patient to the hospital. After the doctor examined him, he said, "Logolanyhulu, your hand and foot are in very bad condition. We may have to amputate one or both of them."

Over the next couple of months, many missionaries and prayer partners in other countries prayed for Logolanyhulu's healing and for his relationship with the Lord.

Several months later, a plane from Missionary Aviation Fellowship flew Logolanyhulu and his family back to the Makki station. Thankfully, the doctor, with God's help, had been able to save his hand and foot, and he would once again be able to walk and use his injured hand. The conflict between the Mursi and Bodi people had ended, so Logolanyhulu and his family were eager to get back to their cattle camp. They had seen the love and compassion of God through the work of the missionaries and the doctor. Logolanyhulu had heard many times what God's Word said about Jesus and how He could change in his life, but he had not yet accepted Jesus as his Savior.

The missionaries continued to pray that one day Logolanyhulu and his family would accept Christ into their hearts. They knew that what God had called them to do was to share His Word at every opportunity and then to pray that hearts would receive His truth. As Jerry and Maija served the Lord in Ethiopia, they often remembered Proverbs 3:5-6, "Trust in the LORD with all your heart and do not lean on your own understanding. In all your ways acknowledge Him, and He will make your paths straight."

QUESTIONS:
1. Why was the "mobile clinic" important for the Mursi people?
2. When Jerry and Maija traveled with the mobile clinic, what else did they do besides provide medical help?
3. Describe the journey of the missionaries to find the Mursi cattle camp.

4. In what ways were the missionaries able to help Logolanyhulu?
5. What did Jerry and Maija believe God had called them to do?

Jerry first went to Tanzania, Africa, as an agricultural missionary in 1962 under the Lutheran Free Church. There he met and married Maija Neuvonen, a missionary nurse/midwife from Finland. Later they served as missionaries in Ethiopia under the American Lutheran Church and as houseparents for missionary children in Cameroon under the Lutheran Brethren Church. After some time in the U.S., they felt called to return to Africa where they began a new outreach to the Mursi people under Sudan Interior Mission (SIM). They are presently retired and living in McVille, North Dakota, where they are members of New Luther Valley Lutheran Church. They have on occasion returned to Ethiopia for short-term mission work.

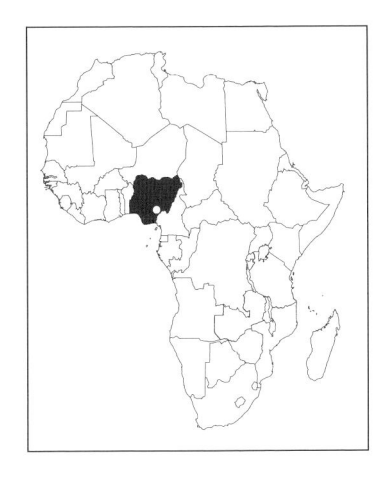

Fire! Fire!

By Elaine Kohl

"Mom! Mom! The fire is coming this way. Will it jump our firebreak and come into our yard?" Kris directed these words to his mother as he and his brother, David, rushed into the house.

Elaine saw the smoke and could hear the fire roaring to the north of the compound where they lived in Ogoja (oh-GOH-jah) Province in Nigeria. It frightened her as she remembered the last dry season when the fire had blown onto the compound as the wind carried it right across the firebreak. The fire had burned across the driveway, but it had not done much harm except for burning a hole in the long plastic hose that carried water from the well to the house.

It was January and the time of "harmattan" (har-meh-TAN), a time during the dry season when the wind blows off the desert to the north. The climate is comfortable then, but the wind dries out the vegetation. Since more than seventy inches of rain had fallen during the rainy season this year, the grass had grown thick and was over six feet tall. There were no cows, horses, or large wild animals to eat the grass because in this area the tsetse (TSET-see) fly spreads disease that kills most animals.

At this time of year, the men of the village often gather together to hunt. To drive out the animals, they will light a fire some distance from the village. Not much thought is given to the direction of the wind or where the fire might go. The fires often burn themselves out, but sometimes the wind comes up and carries the fire along for miles. Sometimes the fires may even burn down a village because the houses are close together with grass roofs, but usually the bare ground around the village will prevent the fire from coming close.

Sigre Unverzagt, age 11

The yard around the mission house was grass, though it had been cut short, not with a lawnmower, but with long knives called machetes (mah-SHET-ees). The grass was brown now instead of green because it had been two months since there had been any rain. The mission house was made of cement block with a metal roof, so it would not burn. However, some of the outbuildings had grass roofs that almost reached the ground. They certainly could catch fire, and then the rafters would burn, and the buildings would be ruined.

As the fire spread through the tall grass around the compound, Elaine knew there was no help except from God. There was no telephone and no fire department to call. Even if she could reach someone on the short wave radio, they would not arrive in time. Her husband, Bob, was away on mission business, so she would have to handle the situation and try to keep the fire from damaging any buildings on the mission compound. Elaine said a quick prayer, remembering Philippians 4:6: "Be anxious for nothing, but in everything by prayer and supplication with thanksgiving let your requests be made known to God."

Then Elaine shouted to the two teenage, household helpers, "Stephen, Maggie, come! We must try to stop the fire. Stephen, fill a bucket with water and bring it here. I'll get some gunny sacks." Because the wind was so strong, it seemed likely that the fire might jump the firebreak.

Meanwhile, Kris and David stood in the yard watching the excitement. Elaine yelled at Kris, "You and David go back to the house. Take care of David and don't come off the veranda."

Kris grabbed David's hand, "Come on, we have to go on the veranda so we will be safe. We can watch from there."

Before long the fire was burning the short grass in the yard. The fire also continued in the long grass beyond the firebreak. It was not easy to work in the smoke, but Elaine and her helpers used their wet sacks to put out the fire while the boys watched from the safety of the veranda. At two and four years old, they were too young to help fight the fire.

The fire was spreading toward the grass-roofed buildings. The three worked frantically to stop the fire. They laid the wet sacks on the burning grass and stomped on them with their feet. Then they slung the wet sacks at the flames while grasping them tightly. Gradually, the length of the line of burning grass grew shorter. Prayers went up as they worked, and their energy was renewed. Finally, they were able to stop the fire just before it reached the grass roofs.

The danger was past, and Elaine, Stephen, and Maggie were exhausted! They returned to the young boys on the veranda. What a sight! All five of them were covered with soot from head to toe. In the excitement, no one had thought to close the windows in the house, so the inside of the house was black with soot too. There were screens on the windows, but they could not stop the tiny, black pieces from coming into the house.

Elaine sat down and gathered the others around her. "Let's pray together," she said. "O Lord, we are so thankful that You helped us get the fire out before it did any damage. Thank You for keeping us from getting burned or overcome with smoke. Amen."

Bob returned at dusk when there was still enough light to see the burnt grass. His heart leaped as he passed the chapel and saw all the buildings still standing. With joy he greeted Elaine and the others, and together they thanked God for keeping them all safe through the fire.

QUESTIONS:
1. Why did the village men start a fire in the grass?
2. Why was the grass so dry in January?
3. What did Elaine do when she saw the fire?
4. How did Elaine, Stephen, and Maggie fight the fire?
5. Who protected Elaine and the others from the fire?

Elaine is married to Robert Kohl, a retired South Dakota State University professor. The Kohl family were lay missionaries in Nigeria from 1963-1966 under the Lutheran Church-Missouri Synod. They live in Brookings, South Dakota, and are members of Calvary Free Lutheran Church, Arlington, South Dakota.

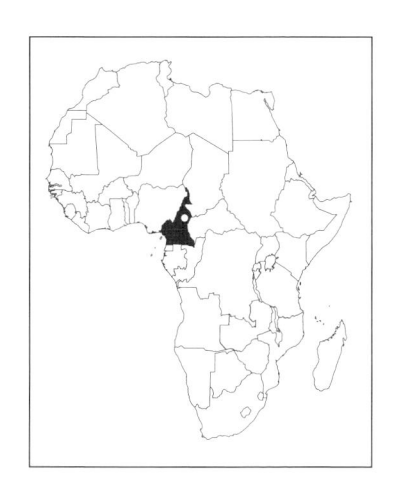

Sowing in Sorrow, Reaping in Joy

By Inez Eikom

The morning sun shone brightly through the small bedroom window of the grass-roofed hut. Mark woke up and gazed outside the window. He marveled at the beauty of the trees, the rocks, and the river. He couldn't help thinking of Colossians 1:16, "For by Him all things were created, both in the heavens and on earth, visible and invisible, whether thrones or dominions or rulers or authorities—all things have been created through Him and for Him."

Suddenly the sickening feeling returned—a gnawing in the pit of his stomach as he remembered what had happened yesterday and why he was back home in his village of Banjuk (Bahn-JOOK). How could he have done this? How could he have disappointed his parents so much? He had failed his exams!

It had been a crushing day. Mark's dream to finish school and make something of himself had been snatched away when the principal of the school approached him, saying they needed to talk.

"Mark, did you find the exam difficult?" inquired the principal.

"No, not particularly," said Mark.

"Well, I'm sorry to have to tell you this news, because your presence at the school is such a blessing," continued the principal. "But there are so many children longing to be educated that we have to maintain a high standard for the students enrolled here. Unfortunately, you failed your exams, which means you will not be able to return to school."

Suddenly, everything was gone! Each step over the many miles he walked back to the village had been painstaking as Mark wondered how he would explain to his parents the reason for his return.

Yes, yesterday had been a very difficult day.

Now he was back with his family in the small village of Banjuk, Cameroon. He was back to do farm work with his father. And somehow the guinea corn, cotton, cassava, and peanuts simply couldn't replace the school and church, and most importantly, his newfound faith in Jesus Christ.

Mark had loved going to school in Tchollire (chohl-LEE-ray). He had started school in a town only five miles from his home village. But in order to go to classes beyond the second grade, it was necessary to go to Tchollire, where all the important government offices were. In these three years while he was away at school, he had learned so much, especially about Jesus, God, and Christianity from the evangelist who lived in Tchollire. God had changed Mark's life in many ways.

As Mark had thought about returning home to Banjuk, he found himself saying a verse over and over: "And we, who with unveiled faces all reflect the Lord's glory, are being transformed into his likeness with ever-increasing glory, which comes from the Lord, who is the Spirit" (II Corinthians 3:18, NIV). Mark wondered if his family and friends in Banjuk would notice the change in him. How would he tell his mother and father that he had become a Christian? Would they understand when he told them he had been baptized?

Six months earlier, fifteen-year-old Mark had accepted an invitation to go to church one Sunday. He had no idea what "church" was and didn't know anything about Christianity. As he sat on the wooden pew, the evangelist had spoken these words: "Once there was a farmer who went to his field to sow his seed." Mark had listened intently as the pastor told what happened to the seed as it fell on four different kinds of soil. The evangelist compared the seed to the Bible, God's Word, and told how it is often hindered from being spread on good and fertile soil. He also shared a verse from John 3:16, "For God so loved the world, that He gave His only begotten Son, that whoever believes in Him should not perish, but have eternal life." That day Mark had received Jesus as his personal Savior. After church, he had told everyone the Good News.

Now back home again and waking up to a new day, Mark recalled the parable that the evangelist had shared and realized that he now must sow the Word of God right here in his own village. He would not only plant guinea corn and peanuts, but he would also share God's Word and help to plant a church.

Emma Twedt, age 13

Mark began by telling his family and friends about Christ. He remembered Matthew 28:19, which says, "Go therefore and make disciples of all the nations, baptizing them in the name of the Father and the Son and the Holy Spirit." His own family responded to God's Word and became Christians.

Within a couple of weeks, a group was meeting together every Sunday morning for worship in Mark's family's house. Six months later, when the group had grown large enough, they decided to build a small, grass-roofed shelter. The chief of Banjuk, who was required by the king to be a Muslim, attended the Christian service often and gave the people a piece of land in the village to build their church. Many people were saved and baptized, and the church kept growing.

Banjuk was a village that had good soil. The Word of God that Mark planted there took root and produced an abundant harvest. As Mark continued to serve the Lord, he claimed Galatians 6:9 as his life verse: "Let us not lose heart in doing good, for in due time we will reap if we do not grow weary."

QUESTIONS:
1. What happened to Mark at the school in Tchollire?
2. How had Mark become a Christian?
3. What gave Mark purpose as he returned to his village?
4. God used Mark to help plant a church. How could God use you to plant seeds of the Word of God?

Inez Eikom grew up with missionary parents in Cameroon, Africa. She left Africa in 1985 to attend college in the United States. Her father and mother, Harold and Ruth Mundschenk, spent thirty-two years in Cameroon and were privileged to nurture the church that Mark started. Inez and her husband, Dan, are members of Emmaus Lutheran Church, Bloomington, Minnesota.

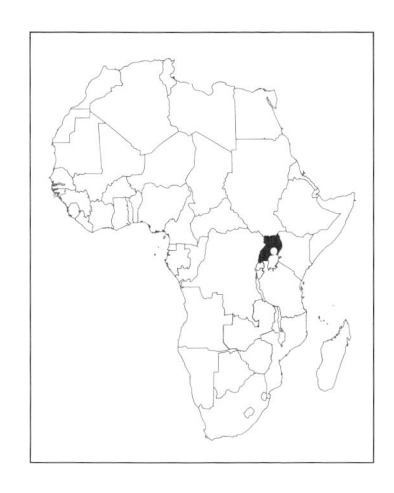

Jonathan and the Little Black Book

By Rhoda Jore

A flash of white skin. Loud, strange talking. Laughter. Images moving back and forth. Jonathan slowed down as he walked along the dirt road, forgetting to watch out for the deep ruts that often made him fall when he was not careful. He peered through the tall fence of the hotel, curious about what he was seeing and hearing. "*Mzungu!*" (muh-ZOONG-goo) he whispered to himself excitedly as he distinguished the face of a white man through a narrow crack. *Mzungu* was the Swahili name for a white person.

In a moment Jonathan found himself leaning up against the fence, anxious for a closer look. There were several white men and women, as well as a large group of Africans. The strangers were teaching the Africans in small groups. They all held an open, black book and frequently pointed to it or read from it. What is that book? Jonathan wondered. The Africans were listening so intently, nodding and smiling, and some of them had black books too. I must find out why those *mzungus* are here and what is so special about that book! Jonathan thought.

Jonathan was twelve years old and just learning to read at school. His family couldn't afford to send him to the village school until this year when his father had found a good job. Jonathan had only seen one book, and it belonged to his teacher at school. She kept it on her desk and would sometimes allow the children to come up and look at the pictures of animals and plants. Jonathan dreamed of having his very own book someday.

"Would you like to come in and listen?"

Jonathan jumped in surprise as he heard a voice behind him. Two women stood looking at him. They both smiled brightly as they waited for his response.

"Come inside and listen," the African woman encouraged in his own language, Swahili.

Jonathan smiled and followed the women inside. They led him to a group of teenagers who were sitting in a circle, listening to a white man read from the black book in English.

The man looked up and smiled as Jonathan sat down on one of the benches. "Welcome!" he said, and then continued to read aloud.

Jonathan knew some English from school but not enough to understand everything that the man was saying. He listened closely, trying to understand as much as possible. He kept hearing three words over and over: "God," "love," and "Jesus." Who is this Jesus? Jonathan wondered. He had never heard that name before. The boy sitting next to him was holding a black book, so Jonathan leaned over to catch a glimpse of it. It was written in English. Jonathan was disappointed. How can I know what they are saying and how can I know who this Jesus is if I can't understand English?

The next day Jonathan came back to the hotel again, hoping that the men and women would be there. They were! This time a woman was gathering a large group of children together. Jonathan excitedly ran over to the area where they were and pushed his way to the front.

He sat down as the woman reached out and touched his shoulder. "Welcome!" she said. Jonathan wondered why the white people were so kind to him and always seemed to be smiling. It was as if they had a special secret. Maybe I will find out what that secret is, he thought.

The woman began to speak in English as she showed them a picture of the world being held up by two hands. Much to Jonathan's surprise, an African woman began to speak in Swahili. As she finished, the white woman continued in English. Then the African woman spoke again in Swahili. Jonathan almost laughed with excitement. The African woman was repeating what the white woman was saying so that the children could understand in their own language! He and the children around him leaned forward to see each picture that was held up, their eyes wide with wonder as they heard the story of a God who created the whole world in six days.

For the next hour, the children sat silently, listening to story after story about God's power and the miracles He had performed. Then, the women began to speak about Jesus. Oh, yes! Jonathan thought. Now I will find out who this man is. He listened attentively as the women

Ryan Jones, age 11

shared about Jesus' life and death. Tears rolled down his cheeks as he listened to them tell about how He was beaten and nailed to a cross. Jonathan smiled happily when they told the good news that He had arisen from the dead. As the women explained more about why Jesus died and rose again, Jonathan felt something stirring in his heart. Was it true what they were saying? Could he know this Man personally and spend eternity with Him when he died?

When the children were dismissed for the day, Jonathan lingered behind. The African woman looked at him and asked, "Would you like to ask Jesus to forgive you for your sins and to be your Savior?"

"Yes, yes!" Jonathan answered without hesitation. The two women knelt with him as he prayed. When he was finished, Jonathan threw his arms around both of them. "I'm so glad you came to tell us about Jesus," he said. "Now I will never again be afraid to die."

As he turned to run home, the white woman reached out and put her hand on his shoulder. "Wait!" she said to him in Swahili. She reached into her bag and pulled out a small, black book. She handed it to him and smiled. He knew it was the same book he'd seen the others holding yesterday. He hugged it tightly to his chest. "Thank you" was all he could manage before tears spilled over onto his cheeks.

Later that day at home, Jonathan pulled out the little black book and opened the stiff, new cover. He gasped as he saw the writing in his own language! This Jesus didn't just speak English, but He could speak Swahili too!

"Thank You, Jesus," Jonathan whispered as he began to read about his new Savior.

QUESTIONS:
1. What did Jonathan see when he peeked through the fence of the hotel?
2. Why did he think that the white people had a special secret?
3. What did Jonathan discover when he opened his little black book?
4. Why do you think it was important for Jonathan to have a Bible in his own language?
5. How can you reach people who speak another language than you?

Rhoda (Monseth) Jore and her husband, Nathan, were part of a teaching team that went to Africa in the summer of 2003, at which time she experienced this story. The Jores sensed God's call to return to Africa as missionaries and began their work in Uganda in 2006, where they continue to serve in the ministry of equipping local church leaders under AFLC World Missions. Rhoda and Nathan graduated from AFLBS in 1999, and Nathan graduated from AFLTS in 2006. They are members of Grace Free Lutheran Church in Maple Grove, Minnesota.

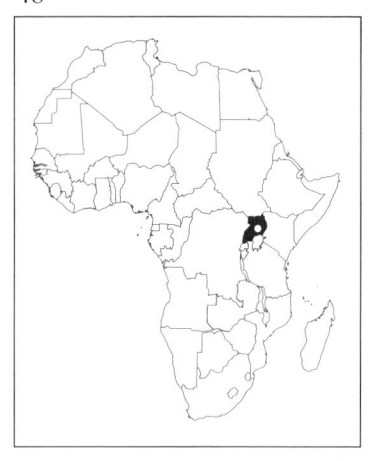

A Visit to Bukoma

By Del Palmer

The heat of the day was beginning to build as four men set out to observe what God was working in the hearts of new believers in the small village of Bukoma (buh-KOH-mah). AFLC World Mission Director, Pastor Del Palmer, had come to Uganda, Africa, to visit the churches there. Today he was traveling to a village forty miles away with Pastor David Natema (NAH-teh-mah), national church president; Pastor Edward Tamale (TAH-mah-ee); and a young man nicknamed "Frenchman."

After several hours of bouncing over ruts and tire-slicing rocks, the men reached Pastor Balise Sospeter's (BAH-lees SOHS-pee-ter's) village. As they met with Pastor Sospeter, it was clear that he was a diligent servant of God. They talked together about evangelism, discipleship, and even Pastor Sospeter's method of constructing church buildings. He was excited about what was happening and suggested to the others that they take a look at the building that had been started a few months earlier.

"The church is just a few miles from here," he said. "Let's all go!"

Everyone climbed into a dusty, four-door sedan and started on the way, driving over what appeared to be little more than a cow path. Everyone was surprised when Pastor David abruptly stopped the car, walked around to the back, and slapped the fender in frustration.

"The tire is flat," he announced, "as flat as it can be!"

Climbing out of the car, Pastor Del remembered the condition of the spare tire that morning when he put his suitcase into the trunk. It was ripped, with cords jutting out of a hole torn open by rocks. Stuck in the middle of Africa, he thought to himself. Now what?

A Visit to Bukoma 49

Undaunted, Pastor Sospeter said, "The church is just behind that grove of trees over there. Let's walk."

As they started walking, a small crowd began to congregate and walk along with them. It became obvious that they were very interested in the white man who had come to their village. Later, Pastor Sospeter said that

Levi Berntson, age 12

Pastor Del was the first white man to visit their village. No wonder the people were so curious.

Soon the church came into view. It had a thatched roof, which was held up by poles to provide shade for the worshipers. It was a wonderful relief to sit down under that thatched roof with the other men and the group that had joined them along the way. Pastor Sospeter explained that the people who had joined them were all members of the congregation that had been started recently.

"Let's pray that the Lord would help us get the tire fixed," Pastor Del said. Several of the men prayed aloud for the Lord's help. As the last "Amen" was uttered, a cell phone rang! One of the men pulled a phone out of his pocket and started talking. Pastor Del's first thought was that it was a line to civilization and help. But the Lord provided help in a more immediate and tangible way.

The group started back toward the car. As the tire was being removed, another sound startled them. This time it was the sound of a motorcycle. Waving and calling, they finally managed to get the cyclist's attention. The tire came off the car, just as the curious motorcyclist arrived to see what was happening.

It wasn't long before the motorcycle left, this time with three passengers—the driver, the muddy tire, and a rider holding the tire sandwiched between himself and the driver.

"Let's go back to the church and have a service while we wait," said Pastor Del. When they got back to the church, there were even more people there. Pastor Edward began leading the children in Christian songs and giving them treats of candy to encourage them. More and more people arrived, eager to be there for the church service.

As the children quieted, Pastor Del preached about God's faithfulness. Reading from Matthew 6:26-27, he reminded everyone that God cares for the birds of the air and cares even more for each person He created. "'Look at the birds of the air, that they do not sow, nor reap nor gather into barns, and yet your heavenly Father feeds them. Are you not worth much more than they? And who of you by being worried can add a single hour to his life?'" As he finished the message, he realized God was seeking to calm his own worries and frustrations, and he gave thanks to the Lord for His timely word.

Then one of the men stood up and shared his testimony. He said, "Before the church came to our community, I didn't know God. Then

Pastor Sospeter told me about my sin and Jesus' sacrifice for me. Jesus saved me. Now I can't get enough of God's Word. I come to church at every opportunity and study the Bible."

As the man sat down, the distant sound of a motor could be heard. It got louder and louder as it came closer. A few minutes later, they heard the car start up, and within seconds it was there at the church. The tire had been fixed. God had provided!

What a great blessing it had been to visit the village of Bukoma and see God's faithfulness in the salvation of souls and in the establishment of a new congregation. As the men said their goodbyes and were getting into the car, one of the villagers grabbed his prized chicken. Handing it to Pastor Del, he thanked him for visiting their village and speaking God's Word to them. Down the road they went: four pastors, "Frenchman," and a clucking chicken.

QUESTIONS:
1. What happened to the men on their way to visit the village of Bukoma?
2. How were they able to get their tire fixed?
3. What should you do when you are in trouble and don't know what to do?
4. What comfort did God give Pastor Del through Matthew 6:26-27?

Pastor Del Palmer is the AFLC World Mission Director and has served congregations in Everett, Washington; Thief River Falls, Minnesota; and Shakopee, Minnesota. He attended AFLBS, and graduated from AFLTS in 1983. Del and his wife, Karen, are members of Faith Free Lutheran Church, Shakopee, Minnesota. The events of this story took place during a visit to several churches in Africa in 2006.

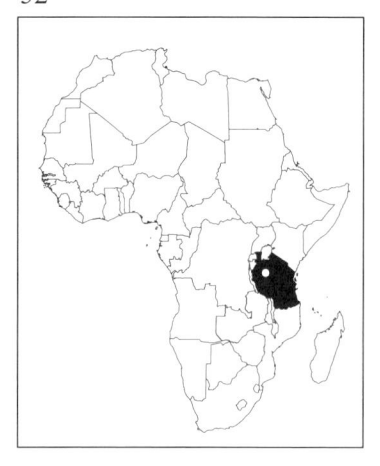

In the Middle of Nowhere

By Kevin Olson

The morning quiet was broken by the sound of a wild donkey braying and strange birds calling. The stars were still visible as the glow of orange appeared in the eastern sky over the Yaeda Chini (Yah-EH-dah CHIH-nee) Valley in northwestern Tanzania. Another day was beginning in this remote, dry area on the African continent. It is the playground of the big animals, where ostrich, wildebeest, impala, elephant, and hyena roam freely.

It's an unusual place for a city boy from Minnesota and his two sons to be camping. "Camping" in this instance means sleeping in the back of a 4-wheel-drive pickup and eating popcorn, crackers, and muffins that Mom had sent along. The Yaeda Chini Valley is the destination of big game hunters, but for Pastor Kevin Olson and his two teenage sons, Nathan and Andrew, this trip had a greater goal. As Jesus had called Peter and Andrew to "Follow Me, and I will make you fishers of men" (Matthew 4:19), Pastor Kevin and his sons were "fishing" for souls to be won for the Lord.

The night before, the Olsons had used the pickup as a generator for electricity to show "The Jesus Film" to the Datoga (dah-TOH-gah) people. It almost hadn't happened, but God opened the way. Earlier that afternoon, they were planning to see the area with two African guides. They wanted to learn more about the culture of the Datoga and their simple lifestyle—how they hunt, farm, and protect their animals. They had planned to be back in plenty of time for the scheduled gathering that evening.

But before they left, they noticed that the engine was getting hot.

Sarah Anderson, age 10

When they lifted the hood, they saw the broken fan belt which was critical to keep the engine cool, charge the battery, and show the movie.

"Now what, Dad?" Nathan had groaned. "What are we going to do out here in the middle of nowhere?"

"Yeah," his brother had agreed. "We're hours from home and miles from anywhere!"

"Well, boys," their father had answered, "it seems that trials like this go hand in hand with our ministry here. Do you remember the flat tire, the dead battery, the overloaded generator, the blown transformer, the flooding, and the smoking extension cord? Do you remember being stuck in the mudhole? Do you remember the heavy rains? But most importantly, do you remember that every time these trials happened, the Lord provided and opened the door for us to continue our ministry?"

Being reminded of God's help through the many difficulties had given courage to them all. After praying together, it seemed best that some of them should stay and wait for people to come for the meeting. The others would drive to the next village, stopping to let the motor cool down as needed, and hoping that the proper-sized fan belt would be available there. It wasn't! But through the ingenuity of the mechanics, a block of wood was wedged between the generator and the engine to hold the oversized belt in place.

"Will that really work?" Kevin had asked the men.

"Of course," they replied.

And it did. Within a short time, they arrived back at the gathering, hooked up the equipment, and projected the life of Jesus on the "screen"—a bed sheet tied to the outside wall of a mud hut. The Datoga people had heard about Jesus for the very first time! They had many questions about who this man was. Some things made sense to them while other things were confusing. They understood the part about the Good Shepherd. Looking for lost sheep was part of their daily lives. But how, they wondered, did He do the miracles? How did He have power over the demons?

"Can He give us bread like He gave the people in the film? Can He forgive our sins? When can we find out more about this person?" they asked.

What a joy it had been for Kevin to read to them from God's Word: "Jesus said to them, 'I am the bread of life; he who comes to Me will not hunger, and he who believes in Me will never thirst'" (John 6:35). And

"For God so loved the world, that He gave His only begotten Son, that whoever believes in Him shall not perish, but have eternal live" (John 3:16).

Now as a new day dawned, they climbed out of the back of the pickup, stretched their cramped legs, and prepared for a good breakfast before starting out for a new place, a new challenge, and a new opportunity to share Jesus. What adventures lay ahead? What trials would there be in this day? They entrusted the answers to the Lord and knew He would be faithful to provide for them no matter what they faced.

Everywhere they traveled with "The Jesus Film," the people came to watch, listen, and learn. The Olsons knew that the reward for this trip was far greater than a trophy to hang on the wall like the reward so many of the big game hunters to the area were seeking. This trip would have an eternal impact, one that would only be revealed fully in heaven.

QUESTIONS:
1. Why were the Olsons sleeping in the back of their pickup?
2. What happened to the pickup?
3. What were some of the other challenges the Olsons had experienced in Tanzania?
4. How did the Lord answer the Olsons' prayer?

Kevin Olson graduated from the Association Free Lutheran Theological Seminary in 1996 and served as AFLC Youth Ministries Director from 1996-2006. He is presently developing a distance-learning program for training pastors in their home countries under AFLC World Missions. This story took place while the Olson family spent several months in Tanzania, Africa, between 2004 and 2005. The Olsons are members of Faith Lutheran Church, Shakopee, Minnesota.

Dear Savior, Bless the Children

Anonymous
Lowell Mason

1. Dear Sav-ior, bless the chil - dren Who've gath-ered here to - day. Oh, send Your Ho-ly Spir - it, And teach us how to pray. Dear Lord, will You please help us O - bey Your great com - mand And send Your bless - ed Gos - pel A - broad through ev - 'ry land?

2. May mis-sion-ar - ies car - ry The mes-sage of Your love, The won-der-ful sal - va - tion You brought us from a - bove. Lord, bless the work we're do - ing, Oh, bless our gifts, though small, And hear our prayer, O Je - sus. You died to save us all.

Savior, While My Heart Is Tender

John Burton
Lowell Mason

1. Sav - ior, while my heart is ten - der, I would yield that heart to Thee; All my pow'rs to Thee sur - ren - der, Thine and on - ly Thine to be. Take me now, Lord Je - sus, take me, Let my youth - ful heart be Thine, Thy de - vot - ed ser - vant make me, Fill my soul with love di - vine.

2. Send me, Lord, where Thou wilt send me, On - ly do Thou guide my way, May Thy grace thro' life at - tend me, Glad - ly then shall I o - bey. Let me do Thy will, or bear it, I would know no will but Thine, Shouldst Thou take my life, or spare it, I that life to Thee re - sign.

3. May this sol - emn con - se - cra - tion Nev - er once for - got - ten be; Let it know no rev - o - ca - tion, Reg - is - tered, con - firmed by Thee. Thine I am, O Lord, for - ev - er To Thy ser - vice set a - part; Suf - fer me to leave Thee nev - er, Seal Thine im - age on my heart.

Asia

Pacific Ocean

RUSSIA

• Petrozavodsk

★ Moscow

Beijing ★

CHINA

Dehli ★

INDIA

Bodduluripadu
Chirala

Indian Ocean

The Fields Are White...

By Jerome Elness

The *Victoria I* cruise ship made its way up the Yangtze River, the longest river in China. A group of sixteen people led by Pastor Jerome Elness were among the three hundred passengers. Pastor Elness was a retired missionary who had spent several years in China. Now he was enjoying seeing the sights of Beijing, the Summer Palace, the "Forbidden City," and the Great Wall with the other passengers. The beautiful scenery and fascinating sights along the river kept them scurrying from one side of the deck to the other in order to capture the best views with their cameras.

At one of the many shops on board, Pastor Elness greeted a young lady selling beautiful, jade and pearl jewelry and colorful, Chinese kites. Speaking to her in the Chinese language, he asked, "What is your honorable family name?"

She answered, "My family name is Zhiang (JYAHNG). I also have an English name, Polly." She paused, then asked, "How is it that you speak Chinese?"

Pastor Elness replied, "I studied Mandarin Chinese in Taiwan and was a missionary there for two years and also in Hong Kong for eight years."

"Oh! You're a Christian pastor," she exclaimed. "I want to become a Christian. Please tell me how to become a Christian now!"

Pastor Elness sensed her excitement and her need to know Jesus. Well, I'd better tell her right now, he thought. So he explained how God sent His Son, Jesus, to reveal His love for us. He told her how Jesus died on the cross in our place to pay the penalty of our sins. He also told her how Jesus rose from the dead on the third day to show His power over sin and death. Then Pastor Elness asked her, "Would you like to pray and ask

Jesus to forgive your sins, acknowledging Him as your Savior and Lord?"

"Yes!" Polly answered. And then, noticing her friend standing nearby listening, she said to her, "Lisa, you'd like to become a Christian, too, wouldn't you?"

Lisa nodded and said, "Yes, I'd like to become a Christian too!"

Pastor Elness led them in prayer, asking Jesus to be the Lord of their lives, to forgive their sins and help them to follow His teachings. Whenever he traveled, Pastor Elness packed New Testaments to give away, so now he gave Polly and Lisa each a bilingual English/Chinese New Testament. He wrote the date they had prayed as well as some promises from God on the inside cover. Taking a highlighter from his pocket, he marked some of the promises in the Bible that dealt with assurance of salvation and the Christian life.

The next day when Pastor Elness saw Polly, he greeted her as "Sister Zhiang" and said, "God bless you today."

Polly responded, "Oh, thank you. I am so happy! I've been reading

Alexia Cardiges, age 9

my New Testament and praying. Last night, I told my roommate I had become a Christian, and she wanted to become a Christian too. I remembered how you prayed with me, and so I prayed with her and shared some of the promises you gave me. Now she is a Christian also." Polly had not even been a Christian for twenty-four hours, but already she had helped two friends come to Jesus and salvation.

Another woman named Joanna who was traveling with Pastor Elness witnessed to Simon, the Chinese guide on the Yangtze River cruise, and to another young man in training. Through Joanna's witness, the Holy Spirit prompted them both to receive Jesus as their Lord and Savior.

Altogether, two young men and four young women on board the cruise ship received Jesus Christ as their Savior and professed a desire to follow His teachings. How glad Pastor Elness and Joanna were that they had enough New Testaments to give to each of the new believers. They also left a "Jesus" video with them in the Mandarin language.

Like many people in China, Polly, Lisa, Simon, and the others had been waiting for someone to tell them about Jesus. Yes, the "fields" along the Yangtzee River were "white for harvest" (John 4:35) as they are in countless places around the world. In Matthew 9:37-38, Jesus told His disciples, "'The harvest is plentiful, but the workers are few. Therefore beseech the Lord of the harvest to send out workers into His harvest.'"

QUESTIONS:
1. Where was Pastor Elness traveling?
2. What did Polly want to know when she found out Pastor Elness had been a missionary?
3. What gift did Pastor Elness give to Polly and Lisa?
4. What happened when Polly told her roommate she had become a Christian?
5. How has God called you to be a worker in His harvest?

Pastor Jerome Elness graduated from Augsburg Seminary in 1957. After studying Mandarin Chinese, the Board of Missions of the Lutheran Free Church sent Pastor Elness and his wife, Elaine, to Hong Kong, China, where they served from 1958-1970. Today he serves Our Redeemer's Free Lutheran Church in Superior, Wisconsin.

Who Lives in Your House?

By Eugene Enderlein

As they entered the village of Bodduluripadu (bahd-duh-luh-ree-PAH-duh) in a remote area of India, Pastor Bussa Yesupadam (BUH-sah YAY-soo-pah-dahm) was explaining to Pastor Eugene Enderlein why Christians here experience so many difficulties.

"We are such a large country," he said. "Only China has more people than India, and there are not many here who believe in the Lord Jesus Christ. Most of the people are Hindu. The Hindu religion has hundreds of gods, which they believe are involved in their lives all the time."

"Tell me about these gods," Pastor Enderlein encouraged.

"Hindus believe that many of the animals are gods," Pastor Yesupadam continued. "So they worship the monkeys, the rats, and even the cobra snake. The Christians in this village want to build a church where they can worship the Lord Jesus. But the Hindus are trying very hard to keep that from happening."

As they approached the home they were planning to visit, Pastor Enderlein asked his friend, "How did Christianity begin in this village?"

"Suseela (soo-SEE-lah), the elderly woman who lives in this house, was the first person in the village to trust in Jesus Christ as her Savior," the Indian pastor responded. "At a time when she was very ill, a Christian lady came to her and prayed for her and taught her about Jesus Christ. She is very devoted to Christ and is a faithful witness to all her neighbors and throughout the village. This has made the Hindus very angry with her. They have done mean and terrible things to her to try to make her turn away from Christ and return to their false Hindu gods. She will tell you herself."

Suseela welcomed the two men into her home. "How has your life been since you became a Christian?" Pastor Enderlein asked her. Pastor Yesupadam served as an interpreter between them since he was the only one there who understood both English and Telugu (TEH-luh-goo).

Suseela's face lit up with joy as she responded, "There is a new radiance within my heart and life. The light of Jesus within me has brought me joy and peace and dispels the fear and dread that filled me when I believed in the false Hindu gods. But it has been difficult to live as a Christian because I have been persecuted by many Hindus in the village."

A cloud seemed to come over Suseela's face, but Pastor Enderlein encouraged her to continue.

"When I went to the town well to draw water," she said, "the other women gathered there made it difficult for me to get near the well." She continued to explain that the well in the village is a gathering place for women to come and socialize with one another. Since she became a Christian, they didn't want her to be with them anymore, so she learned to go to the well at a time when the other women would not be there.

Suseela acknowledged, "Another thing I have had to endure is the damage to my house. At times, there are men and boys who come to my house with very large stones and throw them up onto the roof. The rocks come crashing down through the roof into my house and sometimes break things."

Looking around this simple home, Pastor Enderlein noted it was made of sticks and branches woven together to make a circular wall. A mixture of mud, buffalo dung, and straw had been used to make a plaster that had been spread over the woven stick and branch wall on the inside and outside. The makeshift plaster had hardened much like cement. The roof was constructed of wood beams covered with many layers of palm leaves. It looked like an open umbrella set down on top of the mud walls. He could see that a big rock would do a lot of damage.

Suseela had more to tell. "A strange thing happened to me, for which I praise the Lord," she said. "A cobra snake burrowed into the wall of my house and made its den inside the walls."

Pastor Enderlein felt a little uneasy, knowing that cobras are poisonous. "Oh!" he exclaimed, "and you praise the Lord for that?"

He took a drink of tea and looked around the house. Then he saw where the cobra had taken dirt from inside the walls and had heaped it up into small piles along the top of the wall, just beneath the palm leaves.

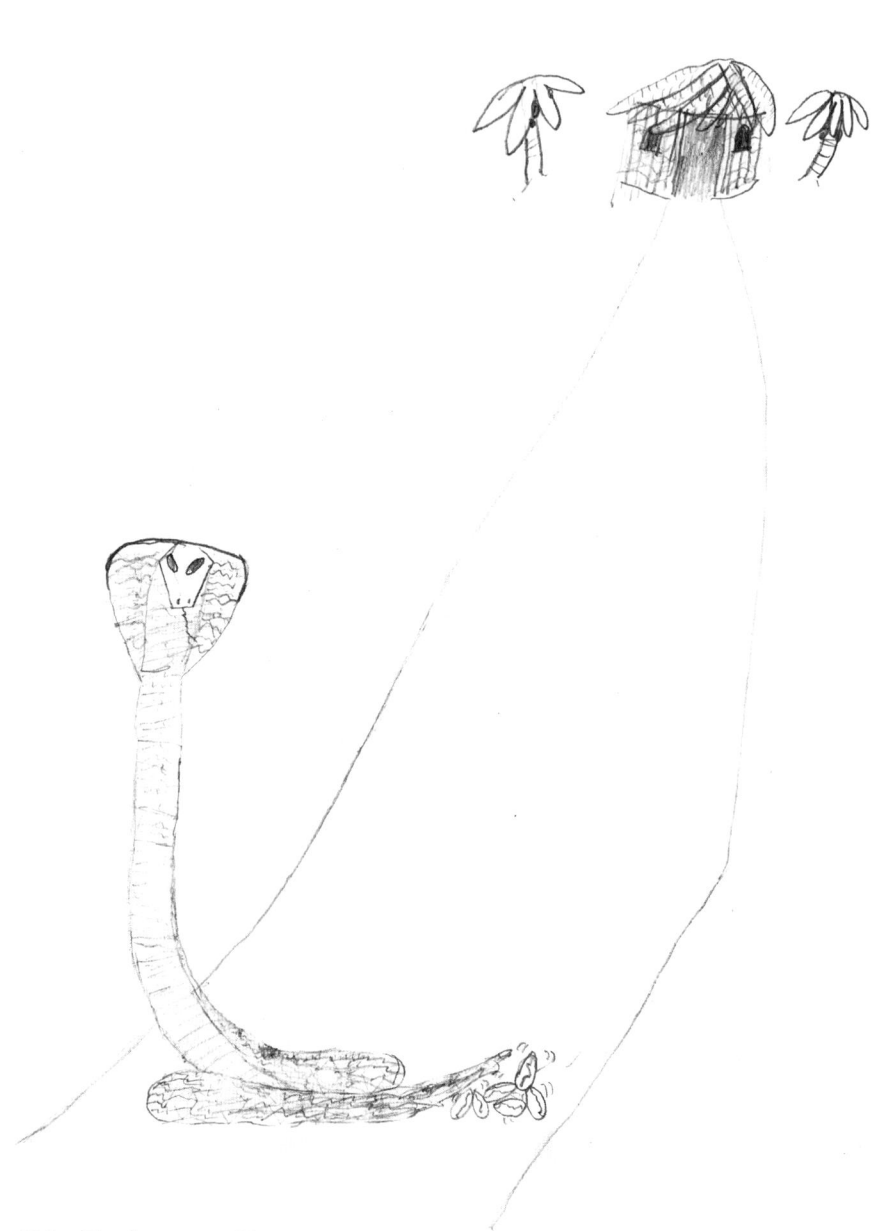

Tyler Erickson, age 12

"The Hindu villagers believe the cobra is a god," Suseela stated, "so they no longer try to damage my house. They even attempted to buy my house from me. I refused to sell it because I know they would turn it into a shrine for the cobra god. I know that God's Word tells me, "'YOU SHALL WORSHIP THE LORD YOUR GOD, AND SERVE HIM ONLY'" (Matthew 4:10).

After praying together with Suseela, asking God's richest blessings upon her, the two pastors left. Neither man said a word for some time. They were deep in thought about this Christian woman who had refused to sell her house, even though the villagers had offered to pay more money than it was worth. Suseela believed in the one, true God and trusted in Jesus Christ as her Savior. She recognized that the cobra was not a god but simply one of God's creatures, and God was using the cobra to protect her from the Hindu villagers.

As they walked along the path to their vehicle, Pastor Enderlein thought about all the people in this remote village who were living in spiritual darkness and did not know Jesus. He remembered Jesus' words in Acts 1:8: "You shall be My witnesses . . . even to the remotest part of the earth." Together the two men prayed that more of the Hindu villagers might come to know Jesus and His wonderful message of forgiveness and eternal life.

QUESTIONS:
1. Why are Christians in India persecuted?
2. How did Suseela demonstrate her faithfulness to Jesus Christ?
3. Why did the Hindu villagers quit trying to damage Suseela's house?
4. In what ways can you show that you are a believer in Jesus Christ?

The events in this story took place on Pastor Enderlein's second trip to India in 1981. The congregation in Bodduluripadu now numbers fifty-five worshipers. They did not have their own church building until February 2007. Before graduating from the Association Free Lutheran Theological Seminary, Eugene Enderlein served with Wycliffe Bible Translators in a technical capacity. After graduation, he served congregations in Minnewaukan, North Dakota, and Thief River Falls, Minnesota. He served as Director of AFLC World Missions from 1979-2002 and has made numerous visits to India, teaching, preaching, and serving alongside the national workers. Eugene and his wife, Beverly, are members of Grace Free Lutheran Church, Maple Grove, Minnesota.

God's Love in Colors

By Karen Palmer

"Good morning, Madam!" called the children as they ran to greet their visitors from America. Eager hands were extended in welcome, and big smiles lit up the children's dark eyes. Surrounded by children of all ages, Karen Palmer and Linda Fugleberg entered the grounds of St. Paul's Lutheran School.

The women were excited to be here! After much planning and anticipation, Karen and Linda were finally in Chirala (chir-AHL-ah), India. They had come to teach the children about Jesus and were part of a team from the U.S. Their husbands had come to teach classes for the national pastors and Bible women.

As the last of the children arrived, a bell sounded, and the students lined up with the smallest children in front and the taller ones behind. Before going to their desks, the children bowed their heads in prayer, recited a pledge, reviewed their verb forms, and sang their national anthem.

The school was a long, L-shaped building covered by a roof of dried palm leaves. On one side, the wall went only halfway up. Three students shared a desk, which was a bench attached to a sloped board for writing. The students listened, memorized, and recited their lessons back to the teacher.

The teacher introduced "Miss Karen" and encouraged the children to listen closely.

"I have a book here without words," Miss Karen began. As the teacher translated, Miss Karen saw the puzzled look on the children's faces. A book with no words? they seemed to question as they looked at each other.

"No words," she continued, "but a wonderful story of God's love all wrapped up in colors. Today's color is gold, and it stands for heaven." Miss Karen told them about God who is in heaven and how He wants each of them to be there with Him someday. She read to them from the book of Revelation, chapter 21, where it describes the streets of heaven made of pure gold. Then she asked them, "Do you want to go there someday?"

The following day Miss Karen sensed the children's excitement as they entered the schoolyard. They were eager to see what the next color would be in the book without words.

"It's black," she said as she held up the book. "Black reminds us of the sin in our heart that prevents us from going to heaven." Then she read Romans 3:23, "for all have sinned and fall short of the glory of God." She saw the crestfallen look on the children's faces. They wanted so much to know that they were going to heaven to be with God.

Wanting to bring them hope, she quickly held up the third color—red. Miss Karen asked, "Does anyone know what the color 'red' represents?" No one raised a hand. She began to tell the children how God still loves them even though they are sinners. From her Bible she read John 3:16: "For God so loved the world, that He gave His only begotten Son, that whoever believes in Him shall not perish, but have eternal life." This, indeed, was good news to the children. Big smiles lit up their faces.

"Red," Miss Karen concluded, "is for the blood of Jesus, who died on the cross for each one of us."

"Miss Karen! Miss Karen!" The excited children greeted her warmly as she entered the school on the third day.

"What is the color for today?" they asked.

Quickly, she took out her book without words and turned to the page for today's lesson.

"It's white," she answered as she held up the book. "White is beautiful because it means that if you believe Jesus died for your sins, He will make your heart clean, turning it from black to white. Jesus wants you to have faith in Him and trust in Him as your only Savior from sin."

Closing the lesson for the day, Miss Karen invited the children to pray with her: "Dear God, I know that I have done many wrong things and have sinned against You. I believe that You sent Your Son, Jesus, to die on the cross for me. Please forgive me and help me to trust in Jesus as my Savior. Amen."

"Tomorrow is our last day together," Miss Karen told the children.

"Be sure to come and hear about the last page in my book. And tell your parents about how much God loves them, too."

The next morning everyone arrived a little early. They were all excited to hear the end of the story. Miss Karen held the book up in front of the children.

"It's green! It's green!" they shouted.

"Yes, it is green," Miss Karen responded. "The color 'green' represents growing things, like the grass, the trees, and the plants all around us.

Bethany Mairs, age 8

We all need to continue to grow in our faith in Jesus."

She then asked the children to hold up one of their hands. "Your hand can help you remember some very important truths about growing in Jesus," she said. "Let's start with our thumb. It points to ourselves and reminds us we need to hear God's Word often." Then she had them point up to heaven, explaining that we need to talk with God every day. She continued, "Our tallest finger reminds us to tell others about Jesus' love." The next finger, the ring finger, was harder to lift up. "Our ring finger cannot stand by itself. Sin in our lives makes us weak. We need to daily confess our sin and ask Jesus to forgive us and strengthen us. The last finger," Miss Karen said, "is the little finger. It is very weak and cannot lift a big pail of water on its own. But when you use all the fingers working together, you can lift the pail. This reminds us to spend time with others who love Jesus who can help us grow in our faith."

"Before I leave, I want to give you something special that will help you remember all the things we have been talking about." Picking up her bag, Miss Karen took out a package. The children strained their necks, trying to see what she had. She drew out a very colorful bracelet with beads of the five colors: gold, black, red, white, and green.

Giving a bracelet to each child, she asked them to wear it every day. "If anyone asks you about your bracelets," she said, "tell them the story of Jesus the Savior." Gladly taking the gift, the children thanked Miss Karen for coming to tell them such a wonderful story.

QUESTIONS:
1. What were the five colors in Miss Karen's book?
2. What does each color represent?
3. Did the children in India understand the "book without words"?
4. Can you recite some of the Bible verses Miss Karen shared?
5. Think of someone you could tell the story of Jesus, using the book without words.

Karen (Pederson) Palmer went to India in January 2007 with her husband, Pastor Del Palmer, AFLC World Mission Director. Karen is a 1973 graduate of AFLBS, and since childhood has had a deep desire to serve the Lord as a pastor's wife or in a missionary capacity. She and her husband are members of Faith Free Lutheran Church, Shakopee, Minnesota.

A New Song in an Old Country

By Don Richman

The door slammed loudly behind Pastor Don and his wife, Mavis, as they entered Lyceum #1 in Petrozavodsk (PET-roh-zah-VODSK), Russia. Hundreds of boys and girls were running in the hallways of the school. Many of them were blonde, blue-eyed, and of course, talking noisily with their friends. Dressed in blue jeans, they looked much like many students in the Midwest.

It was Thursday afternoon, and the Richmans had been invited to attend a boys' choir concert in the school's activity hall. They watched as approximately twenty-five bright, clean, and orderly fifteen-year-old boys filed onto the stage. Silence fell over the hall as everyone waited for them to begin.

How clearly and enthusiastically they sang! Yet the Richmans found themselves feeling sad. Why? Because they knew that most likely all of these boys had been taught atheism—the idea that there is no God. Their teachers, their friends, and even their parents had told them that there is no God.

But this had not always been the case. Russia is an old country that traces its origins back well over a thousand years and a place where Christianity had been established in the tenth century. Since the Russian revolution of 1917, however, atheism had become the official teaching of the whole country. Until now it had been a crime to have a Bible or to believe in God. But now it was 1991, seventy-four years later, and the Communism that had taught atheism in Russia had collapsed. The Richmans were in Petrozavodsk at the invitation of the principal of the school, Juri Shabanov (YUR-ee shah-BAHN-ohv).

Mr. Shabanov with two of his best English teachers had traveled from Russia to Northome, Minnesota, to meet with a group of teachers, hoping to start an exchange program between the two countries. In earlier years, there had been a connection between these two vastly different countries through the iron ore mining industry. Duluth had become a sister city with Petrozavodsk. Because Mr. Shabanov was an atheist and had been active in the Communist Party, his fellow Russians were surprised when he had said to the people in Northome, "Communism has robbed us of our soul. Would you start a Christian Center in my school?"

Helen Bowman, age 16

Pastors and teachers in the Northome area had met together to consider his request. They prayed, "Lord, we have no idea what a Christian Center is or how to start one. What should we do?" Soon they realized that this was an important invitation to proclaim the Gospel of Jesus in an atheistic country. Trusting that God would show them the way, they said "yes" to Mr. Shabanov.

And so Pastor Don and Mavis had come to Mr. Shabanov's school, Lyceum #1, to explore the possibilities of starting a Christian Center. Leaning towards his wife, Pastor Don whispered, "Wouldn't it be great if these boys could sing hymns, choruses, and Scripture songs? Wouldn't it be great if they had a chance to take part in Christmas and Easter plays?" Could that possibly happen? they wondered. Little did they know what God was going to do in Petrozavodsk!

Within three years plans were made, and God miraculously raised up a missionary family from Missouri. Steve and Ann May, along with their four children, moved to Russia. In September of 1995, the Christian Center began in a little room on the first floor of the school. A simple setting with a table, chairs, a teapot, Bibles, Christian books, videos, songbooks, and a computer welcomed students and teachers. They could come any time during the school day, after school hours, as well as evenings and weekends. There was always someone there who would love them and listen to them. Now they could freely hold a Bible in their hands, and they could hear about Jesus!

As the students began coming to the Center, the missionaries noticed that many of them were interested in speaking English. That gave the missionaries an idea. How about starting an English language camp?

Don Bullene, a member of Emmaus Lutheran Church in Bloomington, Minnesota, invited Pastor Richman to visit a mission in Clear Lake, Iowa, that specialized in language camps. The information he learned there, together with language acquisition experience as a missionary in Brazil, helped him to develop a language program for Petrozavodsk.

A group of about forty American Christians came to help teach English at the language camps. Every teacher was given a group of ten Russian students, each of whom received a Bible in Russian and English. The teachers then used the Bible to teach English to the students.

Marina was one example of the 150 students who gathered every morning in the activity hall at 9:00 to sing choruses and hymns of praise in English. A smiling girl in a pretty, white dress, she sat in the front row with her eyes glued on the song leaders. She memorized every word. She repeated every motion. She loved it!

Following a Bible message, the students would go to their classrooms where there would be more singing, studying Bible verses, learning Bible stories, and learning to speak English. Each group was given a Bible story to develop into a skit that they would later present in English to all of the rest of the students, teachers, and workers. Many of the students came to the camps numerous years in a row. Several of them received Jesus as their Savior.

Now after many years, the Friendship English Language Camp (FELC) has spread to other schools in Petrozavodsk as well as to other cities in Russia, Latvia, Slovakia, Poland, and Ukraine. Yes, Russia was closed to the Gospel, but God is faithful, and many are now singing a new song unto the Lord and telling of His glory among the nations (Psalm 96:1-3).

QUESTIONS:
1. Why were Pastor and Mrs. Richman in Petrozavodsk, Russia?
2. Why was it surprising that Mr. Shabanov invited the people of Northome to start a Christian Center in his school in Russia?
3. Describe how the Friendship English Language Camp is an opportunity for students to hear the Gospel.

Pastor Don Richman graduated from Luther Seminary in 1963 and that same year left with his wife, Mavis, for the mission field in Brazil where they served eleven years. While serving as senior pastor of Emmaus Lutheran Church in Bloomington, Minnesota, the Lord called them to begin mission work in Russia and Eastern and Central Europe in 1992. Pastor Richman is the founding director of the East European Missions Network (EEMN).

O Zion, Haste

Mary A. Thompson
James Walch

1. O Zion, haste, thy mis-sion high ful-fill-ing, To tell to all the world that God is Light; That He who made all na-tions is not will-ing One soul should per-ish, lost in shades of night:

2. Be-hold how man-y thou-sands still are ly-ing Bound in the dark - some pris-on-house of sin, With none to tell them of the Sav-ior's dy-ing, Or of the life He died for them to win.

3. Pro-claim to ev-'ry peo-ple, tongue, and na-tion That God, in whom they live and move, is Love: Tell how He stooped to save His lost cre-a-tion, And died on earth that man might live a-bove.

4. Give of thy sons to bear the mes-sage glo-rious; Give of thy wealth to speed them on their way; Pour out thy soul for them in pray'r vic-to-rious; And all thou spend-est Je-sus will re-pay.

5. He comes a-gain: O Zi-on, ere thou meet Him, Make known to ev-'ry heart His sav-ing grace; Let none whom He hath ran-somed fail to greet Him, Thro' thy ne-glect, un-fit to see His face.

Refrain

Pub-lish glad ti-dings; ti-dings of peace; Ti-dings of Je-sus, re-demp-tion and re-lease.

We've a Story to Tell to the Nations

H. Ernest Nichols

1. We've a sto-ry to tell to the na-tions That shall turn their hearts to the right, A sto-ry of truth and mer-cy, A sto-ry of peace and light, A sto-ry of peace and light.
2. We've a song to be sung to the na-tions That shall lift their hearts to the Lord, A song that shall con-quer e-vil And shat-ter the spear and sword, And shat-ter the spear and sword.
3. We've a mes-sage to give to the na-tions That the Lord who reign-eth a-bove Hath sent us His Son to save us And show us that God is love, And show us that God is love.
4. We've a Sav-ior to show to the na-tions Who the path of sor-row hath trod, That all of the world's great peo-ples Might come to the truth of God, Might come to the truth of God.

For the dark-ness shall turn to dawn-ing, And the dawn-ing to noon-day bright, And Christ's great king-dom shall come on earth, The king-dom of love and light.

Europe

Baltic Sea

Jurmala • ★ Riga
LATVIA

Skolnity
Wisla • • ★
Warsaw
POLAND

RUSSIA

Atlantic Ocean

Babushka's Prayer

By Ellen Monseth

Nestled along the Baltic Sea in the cold, north country of Eastern Europe lies a little known nation called Latvia. It is here that Ellen's story begins. It is here that the mothers and fathers and children of families have lived quietly for thousands of years.

The children look much like many boys and girls in America. They also love to play, go to school, and be with their friends. Through the years many hardships have come to this tiny nation, but the children, for the most part, have not been aware of these hardships, except for the sorrows they have experienced in their own families.

You see, for fifty years a strong and powerful nation had controlled this tiny country, depriving them of freedom. This strong and powerful nation was Communist and held the belief that there is no God. They not only believed this for themselves, but they also expected the families of Latvia to do likewise. The churches were closed, many pastors were put to death, and many believers were persecuted for their faith in God.

In 1993—two years after the families of this nation were liberated and given back their freedom—the Monseth family worshiped with some of these families, gathered as a small group of believers at a church that had been closed for those fifty years. Ellen and her husband, Francis, were spending a one-year sabbatical in Eastern Europe, accompanied by their two youngest children, Rhoda and Ben.

As they entered the little, country church that Christmas Eve, they were impressed with the beauty of its simplicity. The church was very cold, with no source of heat. Their eyes were immediately drawn to the few sources of light in the building—an evergreen tree void of decorations except for a few lighted candles decorating its branches and a group of small children standing in a row, holding lighted candles. As she gazed around, Ellen found herself strangely drawn to the face of one little girl whose name was Nikolina.

Nikolina was a small, dainty child, probably around the age of nine or ten. She was dressed quite plainly but was very neat and clean. Her dress was an inconspicuous dark tone that did not detract from the glow of her face and her beautiful, brown eyes. Her hair, dark brown and straight, was shoulder length and tucked back with a simple, dark ribbon. Her legs were covered with the traditional dark stockings, and she wore boots to keep her feet warm. She had a sweet reverence in the way she sang and an awe about her as she listened to the Christmas story of the babe in the manger. This was her first celebration of Christmas in church. She had grown up under the rule of the Communists.

Grace Dryburgh, age 7

Ellen was told that it was Nikolina's *babushka* (buh-BOOSH-kuh), her grandmother, who had taught her the truth that there is a God. It was Babushka who as a young mother herself had kept the faith, secretly teaching her own children and now her grandchildren in the privacy of her home. It was Babushka who had prayed for future generations. Through Babushka, Nikolina had come to know Jesus!

Nikolina's babushka had told her that when she was a young mother some fifty years ago, the very pews they were sitting on in church had been secretly removed in the dark of the night to the loft of a neighbor's barn for safe keeping. Babushka had continued to pray faithfully for the light of Jesus to come back to her people, her church, and her nation. God had answered her prayers, along with the prayers of many babushkas across Latvia. These little women, now frail in body but strong in spirit, had persevered in prayer. Now, dressed in their long dresses, aprons, and kerchiefs, they did not go unnoticed as they ventured out of their homes. They were dearly loved by everyone.

That Christmas Eve, these babushkas demonstrated for the visiting Americans what it truly means to persevere in prayer.

"Then Jesus again spoke to them saying, 'I am the Light of the world; he who follows Me will not walk in the darkness, but will have the Light of life'" (John 8:12).

QUESTIONS:
1. Why had the churches in Latvia been closed for fifty years?
2. What are some blessings those who live in a free country may take for granted?
3. Why was the Monseth family in Latvia on Christmas Eve?
4. What is a *babushka*?
5. How did God answer Babushka's prayer?

Ellen and her husband, Dr. Francis Monseth, along with their two youngest children, spent several months in Latvia in 1993-1994. During that time, Dr. Monseth assisted with the beginning of a Lutheran seminary in Riga, Latvia, and taught pastoral training seminars in Estonia and Russia. Francis and Ellen have returned to Latvia, Estonia, and Russia several times on teaching missions since that time. Dr. Monseth serves as Dean of the Association Free Lutheran Theological Seminary, Minneapolis, Minnesota. They are members of Grace Free Lutheran Church, Maple Grove, Minnesota.

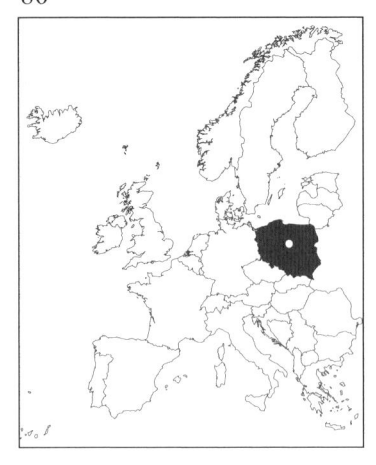

Iwona's Mountaintop Mission

By Tim Hinrichs

As the snowflakes floated down, creating ever increasing mounds of snow, Iwona (ee-VOH-nah) turned from the window. "Do you think the neighbors will be able to come for our special meeting?" she asked her mother, who was finishing some of the food they had been preparing.

"Yes," her mother answered, "they are used to this kind of weather."

Iwona, with blonde hair, brown eyes, and a joyful spirit, seemed to have a word of encouragement for everyone she met. She had been raised in this home in the small community of Skolnity (skohl-NEE-tih), high in the Polish Beskidy mountain range. Life had changed since the fall of Communism, allowing people to speak openly about religion once again. Now in her early adulthood, Iwona had told her parents, "I want to learn more about God. I have heard there is a Bible School in Dziegielow (jeen-GEL-oov), and I would like to go there."

With her parents' permission, Iwona had descended the five-mile, gravel, mountain road to the town of Wisla (VEES-wah), where she had gone to high school and where her parents worked. From there she continued on to Dziegielow by bus. It was only about a thirty-minute ride, but in her anticipation it had seemed like hours driving across the rolling countryside. Upon her arrival at the Bible School, Iwona had been excited as she and the other students were welcomed by two of their new teachers, Pastor Tim and Renata Hinrichs, missionaries with the East European Missions Network (EEMN). Iwona had wondered, What new lessons will I learn here? How will God use me? What can I do for the Lord?

God's Word had touched Iwona deeply as she began her studies and learned so many new lessons. As the class studied the Scriptures, one verse stood out to her. In Matthew 28:19-20, Jesus said, "Go therefore and make disciples of all the nations, baptizing them in the name of the Father and the Son and the Holy Spirit, teaching them to observe all that I commanded you; and lo, I am with you always, even to the end of the age." Iwona meditated on this verse, and she prayed, "Lord, send me as a missionary to others."

Rebecca Jameson, age 11

As the first trimester of the Bible School progressed, God answered Iwona's prayer in a different way than she expected. God directed her thoughts to her own neighborhood in Skolnity, and Iwona had an idea. She told her teachers, "I will organize a New Year's Eve gathering for all my neighbors during the break from school." Pastor Tim and Renata encouraged her as she began to plan this event.

There were no churches in Iwona's hometown of Skolnity, which consisted of about fifty homes. The nearest church was in Wisla, five miles away, and no one ventured that far on Sunday mornings. People in Skolnity knew about God, but very few knew Jesus as their Savior. Deep in thought, Iwona mused, I will evangelize my mountaintop community by inviting them to my home. We will have a large gathering on the occasion of celebrating New Year's Eve!

As soon as Iwona returned home for her school break, she visited every family in Skolnity with a special invitation: "Please come to our home on New Year's Eve for a new kind of celebration!" These hardworking families had been her neighbors for as long as she could remember. She hoped everyone would be eager to come to her home for the New Year's Eve celebration.

Iwona asked her mother and grandmother, "Will you help me prepare the food? Can we make lots of cookies and cakes?" They agreed and also helped Iwona clean the house and clear the veranda for the chairs they would borrow.

As the planning continued, Iwona found someone to play the guitar and lead the singing. She asked a local lay preacher, "Would you bring a message for the New Year's Eve gathering I'm planning?" The preacher agreed to come.

This would be a new venture in Skolnity, and Iwona wondered, What will be the response? Will the people come? She prayed and trusted God who had given her the vision. He would bring in the harvest.

Now the day had finally come, and the falling snow piled up ever higher around all the houses. By evening, the houses looked like picture postcards with three feet of snow blanketing the rooftops. Walkways between the houses seemed like tunnels in places. Would anyone come to the celebration?

"Look, Mother! Look, Grandmother!" shouted Iwona excitedly. "The people are filling the tunnels and coming to our house!"

Soon the chairs along the veranda were filled with the neighborhood families and people overflowed into the other rooms. Excitement filled the rooms as the people listened to the Gospel songs and joined in when they knew the words. Then a silence came over them as the preacher shared a message about having a relationship with the Lord Jesus Christ. This was something new to many, and others hadn't heard this message in a long time. Seeds were being planted as this little community was drawn together by the Word of God.

God had answered Iwona's desire to be a missionary by calling her to go to the mission field of her own home community, a place unreached by any church and a place which needed to hear the Gospel. Now the moment was right, and the community flocked together at Iwona's invitation.

Iwona continued to follow God's call and organized more events in the following years for the community of Skolnity in their home. Often nearly seventy people gathered together. Iwona also started a Bible study, and people began to grow in their faith and in their love for Jesus the Savior. Some began returning to the church in Wisla, making the long, five-mile trek down the mountain on Sunday mornings. The community began to come alive again spiritually after so many years of living far from a church and far from God.

After Iwona married, she and her husband built a house with a special design that included a large meeting room for outreach to their neighbors. They continue to be missionaries in their own community.

QUESTIONS:
1. How did God lead Iwona to a different mission calling than she expected?
2. What invitation did Iwona give her neighbors in Skolnity?
3. What happened after the first gathering at Iwona's home?
4. What groups of people do you know who have not yet been reached with the Gospel?
5. How could God use you to serve the needs of people in your own community or neighborhood?

Pastor Tim and Renata Hinrichs began serving as missionaries in the Czech Republic in 1995 and have been serving in Poland since 2001. They are presently directing the Bible School for the Lutheran Church of Poland in the southern village of Dziegielow. Tim, a graduate of the Association Free Lutheran Theological Seminary, grew up in Hartland, Minnesota. Renata is from Bielsko-Biala, Poland, which is thirty miles from Ustron where they presently live. On loan from AFLC World Missions, they are working with the East European Missions Network.

I Love to Tell the Story

A. Catherine Hankey
William G. Fischer

1. I love to tell the story Of unseen things above, Of Jesus and His glory, Of Jesus and His love. I love to tell the story, Because I know 'tis true; It satisfies my longings As nothing else could do.

2. I love to tell the story; More wonderful it seems Than all the golden fancies Of all our golden dreams. I love to tell the story, It did so much for me; And that is just the reason I tell it now to thee.

3. I love to tell the story; 'Tis pleasant to repeat What seems, each time I tell it, More wonderfully sweet. I love to tell the story, For some have never heard The message of salvation From God's own holy Word.

4. I love to tell the story; For those who know it best Seem hungering and thirsting To hear it, like the rest. And when, in scenes of glory, I sing the new, new song, 'Twill be the old, old story, That I have loved so long.

love to tell the sto-ry, 'Twill be my theme in glo-ry To tell the old, old sto-ry of Je-sus and His love.

And Jesus came up and spoke to them, saying,

*"All Authority has been given to Me
in heaven and on earth.
Go therefore and make disciples
of all the nations,
baptizing them in the name of the Father
and the Son and the Holy Spirit,
teaching them to observe
all that I commanded you;
and lo, I am with you always,
even to the end of the age."*

Matthew 28:18-20

North America

"What Can I Do?"

By Clara Gunderson

The child sat still, though most of the others had left the room. She was unaware of the activity around her, lost in the exciting story she had just heard. As Mrs. Erickson observed her, she could tell that the child was deeply moved, and she went over and sat down beside her.

Janie turned to her with a puzzled look and asked, "What can *I* do?"

They were sitting in the basement of Trinity Lutheran Church, the church Janie and her family attended. Mrs. Erickson had just finished telling the Sunday School about living and working as a missionary in Bolivia. It was hard for Janie to understand *where* Bolivia was, but it was even harder to understand *why* the people there didn't know Jesus. *Why* the children there didn't know Jesus.

Janie had always known about Jesus. She knew wonderful stories about His life: how He helped everyone, healed terrible diseases, and talked about His Father God, who had created the whole world. Why, she had even heard how He had made a friend that was dead come alive again!

Mom and Dad took Janie and her sisters to Sunday School and church every Sunday, and she loved to sing the songs. She had picked one as her very favorite: "My Jesus, I Love Thee, I Know Thou Art Mine."

But now, for what seemed to be the first time, she had heard that there were children—and their moms and dads—who didn't know Jesus. Many had never had a chance to hear the wonderful Bible stories.

As she sat beside Mrs. Erickson and asked what she could do, Mrs. Erickson told her that she could pray every day that the Lord would send more people to Bolivia and to other places to tell about Jesus' love for

Susan Welsch, age 17

them. To tell how He wanted all people everywhere to love Him and be His children, to go to live with Him in heaven forever.

Picking up her Bible, Mrs. Erickson said, "Janie, I want to read a special part of God's Word to you. It may be hard for you to understand, but listen as I read and then I'll explain it." Turning to Matthew 9:37-38 she read: "Then He said to His disciples, 'The harvest is plentiful, but the workers are few. Therefore beseech the Lord of the harvest to send out workers into His harvest.'"

"Janie, that means that there are many, many people who are ready to hear the story of Jesus, who died for their sins, but there are only a few who are going to tell them. Jesus tells His disciples to pray that people will go and tell the story of salvation. Do you understand?"

"Yes," Janie promised, "I will pray that prayer!"

Over the next few years at church and at Bible Camp, Janie had many more opportunities to hear missionaries tell about their work in Africa, India, Ecuador, and Mexico. They showed slides of the people—some sitting in a little church, some sitting outside on the grass, some getting help because they were sick, and some whose babies had died because their parents couldn't get help in time. Most wonderful of all would be the stories of how the people would come to know Jesus as their Savior. Through all of this, Janie remembered her promise to pray that more people would go and tell the story of Jesus' wonderful love.

QUESTIONS:
1. What did Janie learn that day from Mrs. Erickson's talk?
2. Why was she surprised about what she had learned?
3. What did she promise to do?
4. Will you pray for more missionaries to go and tell about Jesus' love?

"Janie" in this story is Clara Gunderson. Clara and her family served in Bolivia under the World Mission Prayer League (WMPL) from 1967-1976. They also served under WMPL in Mexico for eleven years. Her husband, Richard, graduated from the Association Free Lutheran Theological Seminary in 1967 and today serves as Assistant to the President of the AFLC. They are members of Sunnyside Free Lutheran Church, Stacy, Minnesota.

"Nothing Shall Hurt You"

By Linda Haabak

"Stop! Stand still!"

Betty froze. "What's wrong?" she asked, beginning to turn around.

"Don't move! There's a rattlesnake beside the trail—about eighteen inches from my foot," Linda responded.

Betty slowly turned her head to look behind her. "Ohhh, he's so big!"

"Yes, he is, and I'm surprised that he didn't strike. This one must be sleeping soundly. Maybe he just had a good meal. They say the first hiker wakes the snake up, and the second hiker gets bitten. And I'm probably allergic to one of the ingredients of snakebite antivenin. If the bite didn't kill me, the antidote might."

The young women stood motionless for a couple of minutes, watching the rattler sprawled in the sunshine. They could hear the rest of the group on the conditioning hike approaching behind them. The snake, roused by the vibrations of twenty hikers' footsteps, slithered away into the underbrush. The rattles on his tail made a soft sound each time they moved from side to side.

That evening Linda visited with her friends. In a few days, she would leave them to go to Wycliffe Bible Translators' Jungle Training Camp in southern Mexico. It was late when she retired to her dorm room, and her roommates were already asleep. What should she do? She had changed her bedding that day and wanted to take a shower before sleeping between the clean sheets. But a shower would wake her roommates. So Linda grabbed the extra blanket from the foot of her bed and wrapped up in it on the floor.

Early the next morning, Linda woke with a start. What was that strange lump under her pant leg? She gently traced the dimensions—about an inch long and a quarter inch wide, throbbing strangely. Linda sprang to her feet and rushed into the walk-in closet, closing the door and fumbling for the light switch. She whipped off her jeans and investigated her leg and the floor. Nothing. She gave her trousers a couple of hard shakes. There! A scorpion! Linda grabbed her hiking boot and dispatched the critter, murmuring, "And that strange throbbing was you trying to get your tail over your head so you could sting me. If my pant leg hadn't been in the way, you would have!"

Luke Quanbeck, age 16

Later that day Linda read her devotions, continuing in Luke where she had left off the day before. Her heart leapt when she read the nineteenth verse of chapter ten: "Behold, I give unto you power to tread on serpents and scorpions, and over all the power of the enemy: and nothing shall by any means hurt you" (KJV).

"Thank You, Lord, for the snake and the scorpion and for the encouragement from Your Word," Linda prayed. "You know my tendency to fear the unknown and the dangers I might face in Mexico. Thank You for assuring me of Your presence and protection."

With a light heart, Linda finished the week of orientation in Dallas, Texas, and headed for a five-month adventure south of the border, reminding herself often of the Lord's goodness to her.

QUESTIONS:
1. What was the first danger Linda encountered?
2. Why do you think the rattlesnake didn't strike her?
3. What danger did Linda encounter next?
4. Why couldn't the scorpion sting her?
5. Why was the Bible verse in Luke such an encouragement?

Linda grew up near Kloten, North Dakota, receiving Christ as her personal Savior at age sixteen. She graduated from AFLBS in 1970 and from Mayville State College in 1972. After teaching elementary school in Alsen, North Dakota, Linda joined Wycliffe Bible Translators in 1974. She served in Africa for a short time in Cameroon and Côte d'Ivoire (Ivory Coast) and has served about thirty years in Wycliffe offices in the U.S. She is a member of New Luther Valley Lutheran Church in McVille, North Dakota.

Border Crossing

By Todd Schierkolk

On the morning of their planned departure to Mexico, Todd and Barb awoke feeling tired and very nervous. There was still so much to do. But they were also very excited. The day had finally come to move across the border into Mexico and begin their missionary service!

Three friends had arrived the day before from El Campo, Texas, with their pickup and a trailer, which had already been loaded. The sun was just coming up as they all gathered together to pray: Todd and Barb with their two half-asleep little girls, Rachel and Megan, and the three friends. They asked the Lord for safety and blessings as they began the ten-mile trip to the border. What excitement! They were actually leaving for Mexico. They made their own mini parade as they pulled out onto the street—the family in a white sedan and the three men in a maroon pickup pulling a rusty, gold trailer.

As the bridge came into view, Todd's heart started pounding, and he began to pray. He paid the toll and drove onto the bridge, looking down at the Rio Grande River, the border between the United States and Mexico. Soon he was rolling down his window to speak to the Mexican border guard with his "fresh-out-of-language school" Spanish. The guard asked where they were going and what they were carrying. Todd pulled out his papers and showed him the baggage list he had carefully prepared. He was motioned forward to the stoplight which "randomly" selects who will be inspected and who may freely pass. For them it flashed red—STOP!

While the others waited by the vehicles, Todd was sent from one office to another, each time being told he couldn't enter Mexico. He knew he had all his papers in order. He had read all the Mexican regulations about entering. Yet here he was, being refused entry. Discouraged, they had to return to the retreat center they had left that morning on the United States side of the border, not knowing what to do next. But they knew that God had called them to this work in Mexico, and they would not give up!

With many people praying and with some strategic counsel from people at the retreat center, the group set out once again the next morning, with renewed hope and excitement. Once again they were stopped at the border for inspection. After three hours, Todd was taken to an office to calculate the amount of tax they would have to pay on the things they were bringing into the country. There he met the "administrator," who was surprisingly young and casually dressed. Todd noted that he was wearing a Michigan Wolverines cap and asked if he was a basketball fan. As the final calculations were being made, they chatted about different things, and Todd felt he had finally met someone who could understand their situation.

Hannah Peterson, age 10

"My name is Caesar," he told Todd as he handed him the bill. "Tell them at the next checkpoint that the administrator at the border checked you out and calculated your taxes."

Unfortunately, Todd didn't realize the importance of this man's name until it was almost too late.

What relief and excitement they felt as they pulled away from the border. And they were thankful to the Lord who had heard the prayers of all the people back home. But their excitement was tempered somewhat by the realization that they still had to pass through another checkpoint a short ways down the road.

"Kilometer 30," the second checkpoint, was a safety net of sorts. Whatever gets by the scrutiny of the guards at the border is hopefully caught by the officials at Kilometer 30. When they arrived, they were immediately waved over to a parking area. Todd's stomach was churning as he gave the guard all of their papers and told him, "The administrator at the border told me to tell you he had checked us out and calculated the taxes himself." The guard appeared not to have heard and ordered Todd to unload everything. Todd's heart sank!

It soon became apparent that this stop was going to be difficult. As Todd and his friends unloaded boxes and barrels, the guard began checking the list against the contents. With a Swiss Army Knife, he began cutting the tape on each of the sixty-five boxes. He was irritated and let Todd know it. He challenged Todd on the value of many items. When Todd tried to respond, the guard cut him off. Todd found out that his beginning Spanish was not adequate to deal with this situation. The crowning humiliation came when they opened Barb's suitcase. Everything fell out on the ground.

Todd felt defeated as he and his friends began repacking the boxes and suitcases. How grateful he was to have these friends along, not just because of the physical help but also for their silent encouragement to hang in there and not give up. Finished packing, Todd walked over to the office where the guard was talking to his supervising officer in frustrated and tense tones. He was told to stand on the other side of the driveway. When the officers finished talking, Todd was waved into the office.

He wouldn't remember everything that was said to him in that office, but he was beginning to realize that the whole incident had nothing to do with what their boxes contained. It had nothing to do with paying the taxes. It was about the power this guard felt in telling him what to do. It was about his power to tell him, "No, you can't come into Mexico."

Calm now in this realization, Todd said the same thing he had said before: "The administrator at the border told me to tell you that he had checked us out himself and personally calculated the taxes."

The guard looked at Todd and exclaimed, "The administrator! The administrator! Who is this administrator? Do you know him personally?"

"You mean his name?" Todd asked. "You mean, Caesar, the basketball fan who wears a cap that says, 'Michigan Wolverines'?"

He stared at Todd, dumbfounded. Then one of the guards called "the administrator" back at the border to verify Todd's story. Yes, "the administrator," Caesar, had said they could pass. In two minutes it was all over. Their papers were approved; they could go!

It has been several years since that adventurous border crossing in 1995. And in that time, the Schierkolks have seen many more answers to prayer. Their hearts are filled with gratitude to God who has called them and chosen to accomplish His will through the prayers of His people even as He helped them at that border crossing so many years ago.

"What then? Only that in every way, whether in pretense or in truth, Christ is proclaimed; and in this I rejoice. Yes, and I will rejoice, for I know that this will turn out for my deliverance through your prayers and the provision of the Spirit of Jesus Christ" (Philippians 1:18-19).

QUESTIONS:
1. Who were the Schierkolks' helpers in this story?
2. What were some of the difficulties they encountered trying to cross the border?
3. How did God answer their prayers?

Pastor Todd Schierkolk and his wife, Barb, have served as missionaries in Mexico under AFLC World Missions since 1995. He graduated from Concordia College, Moorhead, where he met his wife, Barb. He graduated from the Association Free Lutheran Bible School in 1987 and from the Association Free Lutheran Theological Seminary in 1992. Before going to Mexico, he served as pastor of Ebenezer Lutheran Church, Evergreen Park, Illinois, from 1992-1995.

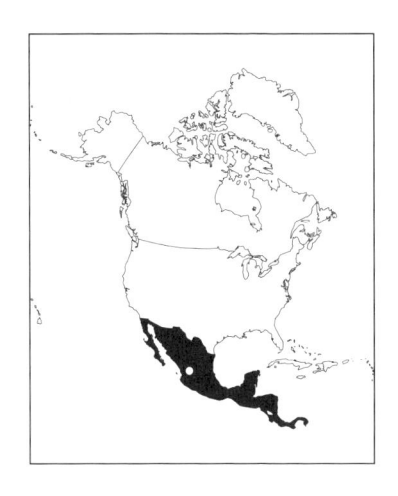

Mario and Viki

By Todd Schierkolk

Mario loved basketball. Whenever he could get away, he would go to the neighborhood court for a pickup game of basketball. One day when he went to the court, he met a group of young people form the United States who had come there looking for the same thing. Introducing themselves to one another, they formed teams and the game began.

The young people had come to Jerez (heh-REZ), Zacatecas, Mexico, from Medicine Lake Lutheran Academy in Minneapolis, Minnesota. They were there for two weeks to work alongside the missionaries, the Todd Schierkolk and Dan Giles families. Exercise and fun weren't their ultimate goal that day. They wanted to meet the neighborhood families and invite them to their presentations.

Mario eagerly responded to the invitation to come to one of their programs at a local high school. He and his wife, Viki, were impressed as they watched the young people do a pantomime of the crucifixion and resurrection of Jesus and of Satan's efforts to undermine God's plan to save the world. Wanting to know more, Mario and Viki went to the presentations at the other high schools as well, where the team dramatized the Gospel through synchronized movements, puppets, music, and the Word of God.

After the team returned to the U.S., Pastor Todd hoped to keep in contact with Mario. So when Mario invited him to join a basketball league, he gladly accepted. They continued playing together every week for several months, and the two families became good friends.

Rachel, the Schierkolks' oldest daughter, cared deeply for the children and youth of Jerez. She invited Saudit (SOU-dee), Mario and Viki's daughter, to come to church. Saudit accepted the invitation and asked her cousin, Jocelyn, to come too.

So Pastor Todd, his wife, Barb, and their three girls picked up Saudit and Jocelyn on Sunday mornings and brought them to the worship service and Sunday School. During the Sunday School class one week, Saudit prayed with her teacher, Debbie Giles, asking Jesus to come into her heart and to be her Savior.

One Sunday morning soon afterwards, the whole family—Saudit and Jocelyn, Mario and Viki, along with their son, Junior—were waiting on the curb as the Schierkolk van pulled up. Rachel smiled in delight at her father. What an answer to their prayers!

That Sunday, Pastor Dan Giles shared with them from Romans 10:9, "that if you confess with your mouth Jesus as Lord, and believe in your heart that God raised Him from the dead, you will be saved." Both Mario and Viki prayed that day to receive Jesus as their Savior.

The change in them was dramatic! They were new people after trusting Jesus for their salvation. "Therefore if anyone is in Christ, he is a new creature; the old things passed away; behold, new things have come" (II Corinthians 5:17).

Mario and Viki owned a tortilla shop in Jerez. As a staple food in Mexico, tortillas are in demand every day of the week, Sunday included. But Mario and Viki wanted to be in church to worship their Savior on Sundays. So together they made the decision to close their shop on Sundays, and God honored their decision. Their business actually improved, and they began earning more money even though they were working one less day.

Junior noticed the dramatic change in his parents. His mother had a radiant smile and a much softer nature. His father spent more time with the family, and he didn't hit the kids like he had before.

The family continued attending weekly church services together, hearing God's Word. One Sunday morning when they arrived at church, Junior was in great pain because of a kink in his neck. He could hardly move his head. After the church service, there was a picnic dinner in the nearby park, followed by a time of singing and praying. Then the congregation gathered around him, Pastor Giles laid his hands on him, and they prayed for God's healing. The healing came in a dramatic way.

As the family walked home after the picnic, they passed by a shop that had a low-hanging awning over the door to keep out the sun. Junior didn't see it and smacked his head hard. As he recovered from the shock of hitting his head, he moved it around and realized that the kink was gone! The family talked about that dramatic answer to prayer for several weeks, and it played an important part in helping Junior realize that the God of the universe was really interested in him. After the Sunday worship service several weeks later, Junior also became a Christian, trusting in Jesus as his Savior.

David Peterson, age 7

QUESTIONS:
1. What did the team from Medicine Lake Lutheran Academy do that interested Mario?
2. How did Pastor Todd continue to build a friendship with Mario after the team left?
3. What important thing did Rachel do?
4. What happened that helped Junior realize that God was interested in him?
5. How can you build friendships with people around you to help others come to know Jesus?

Pastor Todd Schierkolk and his wife, Barb, have served as missionaries in Mexico under AFLC World Missions since 1995. He graduated from Concordia College, Moorhead, where he met his wife, Barb. He graduated from the Association Free Lutheran Bible School in 1987 and from the Association Free Lutheran Theological Seminary in 1992. Before going to Mexico, he served as pastor of Ebenezer Lutheran Church, Evergreen Park, Illinois, from 1992-1995.

A New Life for Virginia

By MaryAnn Jackson

Carlos tried hard to steady his bike as he navigated around the deep potholes in the muddy street.

"Mud, mud, mud!" he muttered. "Mud everywhere!"

He was on his way home after a long day's work in the city of Puebla (Poo-EB-lah) in southern Mexico. "Loma Bonita" or "Beautiful Hill" was the name of his *colonia* or neighborhood on the outskirts of the city.

"It's more like "Loma Lodo," he said out loud. "More like a muddy hill than a beautiful one!"

Most of the people living here had come from one small village or another in hopes of a better life because there was work to be found in the big city. Most had hopes of one day returning to their village where their extended family lived. They had left behind parents, grandparents, aunts, uncles, cousins, and in-laws. Carlos had left his wife and children in Huahuaxtla (wah-WASH-tlah) until he could find a piece of land and build a house.

Now as he neared home, he was so glad that he had finally been able to bring his family to the city so they could be together again, even though there was much work yet to be done on his house. He knew his wife was very lonesome for her village, where folks had time to stop and visit and where there were fewer cars and trucks, no smog, and no crowds.

So far there were no churches in Loma Bonita. And taking his wife and little ones on the city bus to the church in San Miguel (sahn mee-GEL) each week meant a two-hour ride each way. So Carlos had invited the folks from the congregation in San Miguel to start a church in his home in Loma Bonita.

Tonight he was excited to get home because Pastor Darwin and Miguel (mee-GEL), a young man from the church, were coming to have an evangelism class with him. Part of the course was going door to door sharing the Gospel, inviting their neighbors to accept Jesus as their Savior.

The men were eagerly waiting for him when he got home. "Let's pray before we go out tonight," Darwin said, "that God will lead us to someone who is ready to receive Jesus."

Ross Ackerman, age 10

After praying, they went out into the neighborhood. They spoke with many people who wanted to talk and argue about religion and the Bible but who didn't want to talk about their need of Christ. They didn't want to give up their sins and follow Jesus.

"It's getting dark," Carlos said, "and people are afraid to open their doors at night. Maybe we'd better go back home."

The others agreed. But as they headed back to Carlos's house, they saw a group of men sitting in a yard. They stopped to talk with them, hoping for a chance to tell them about the love of Jesus. The men had been drinking. Nevertheless, they listened politely as Darwin told them the Good News.

On the way home, Miguel voiced what they were all thinking: "They'll probably not even remember any of it by morning."

After arriving back at Carlos's house, they prayed for all the people they had spoken with that evening, asking the Lord to water the seeds they had planted.

The next week after class, they were excited to begin their visits again.

"Let's get going!" said Miguel. "I wonder what the Lord has done this past week in the lives of the people we spoke with."

"Well," Carlos replied, "the Lord promises that His Word will not return empty, that it will work in the hearts of the hearers."

The three men prayed and started out for the evening. Tonight no rain hindered their walk, and the air was warm and lovely. After a while they ended up back at the house where the group of men had been gathered the prevoius week. The house belonged to a man named Ezequiel (ee-ZEE-kee-uhl). Virginia, Ezequiel's daughter, came out and spoke to them through the gate.

"No, my father isn't home," she told them.

Disappointed, Darwin answered, "We'll try to come back next week," as they turned to leave.

"Wait!" cried Virginia. "When you came last week and were speaking to my father and his friends, I was listening. I believed what you said."

The men praised God. Virginia had received the Lord! They shared Scripture with her and prayed, leaving a New Testament in her hands. She told them how her life had been so miserable. She had felt so empty inside, longing to know what was the matter. But when she heard the men talking to her father about the Lord, she knew that this was what she longed for.

Before the men left, they invited her to the church service the next Sunday. Virginia came. She could see that this was what her father needed also. After telling her father about it, he came with her the following Sunday.

Ezequiel told them that his father had been a preacher. At one time Ezequiel, too, had trusted Christ as his Savior. He had been working in construction. Since just about everything in Mexico is made of bricks or concrete blocks, it meant a lot of heavy lifting. He was tired and just couldn't lift the buckets of wet cement anymore. Life had gotten him down, and he turned to drinking with his buddies to ease the pain. Now he wanted, with all his heart, to return to Christ and live for Him.

Both Virginia and Ezequiel began coming to church every Sunday. Often Ezequiel would pray: "Dear Lord, thank You for sending someone to show me that I was lost without You. I am eternally grateful to You and to my new friends." Virginia became a Sunday School teacher and later took the evangelism class. In their excitement and thankfulness, Virginia and Ezequiel began sharing the Good News with others.

"How then will they call on Him in whom they have not believed? How will they believe in Him whom they have not heard? And how will they hear without a preacher?" (Romans 10:14).

QUESTIONS:
1. Why was Carlos eager to get home from work?
2. What had Carlos asked the congregation in San Miguel to do?
3. How was Virginia an answer to Darwin's prayer?
4. Do you think you need to take an evangelism course before you can tell others about Jesus' love? Why or why not?

Darwin and MaryAnn Jackson are members of Elim Lutheran Church in Lake Stevens, Washington, where they became Christians under the preaching of God's Word. In 1995 they sensed God calling them into full-time mission service. In 1997 they arrived in Mexico under the auspices of the World Mission Prayer League, where they continue to serve.

"We Are Praying for You"

By Karen Knudsvig

At a very early age, Karen became especially interested in missionary stories and asked many questions. Missionaries would often come to Our Saviour's Lutheran Church to tell about their work on the mission field. Pictures of the missionaries were displayed in a special place at church, and Karen's Sunday School teachers regularly encouraged the children to pray for the missionaries and their families.

A few days after her twelfth birthday, Karen was walking through the trees surrounding their farm yard near Page, North Dakota. It was a warm summer day. As she approached their big, white farm house, she saw her mother, Myrtle, sitting alone on the porch, enjoying the cool breeze and the beauty of God's creation. Karen listened to the familiar hymns that her mother was humming and went to sit down beside her.

"Did you have a nice walk?" Myrtle asked her daughter.

"Yes," Karen responded, "and I've been thinking about what I want to be when I grow up. I keep thinking about all the hungry people in the world and all those who haven't heard about Jesus."

"Would you ever like to be a missionary?" her mother asked.

Karen looked at her mom and said, "I'm not sure, but I do think about it often."

Looking into her daughter's eyes, Myrtle reminded Karen that she was a missionary for Jesus right now by praying for the hungry people in the world and for the missionaries and by giving money in the monthly mission offerings.

"You know, Mom, that's what our pastor and Sunday School teachers say too. We are all missionaries and are little lights for Jesus."

"That's right," agreed her mom. "When you help others and tell your friends about Jesus, you are being a missionary!"

Then Karen asked, "How will I know if I am to be a missionary to another country?"

"It is important to pray every day and ask Jesus to guide you," her mother said. "I want you to know that I pray every day for you and your brothers and sisters, that you will always follow Jesus. Now look, your brothers are going to the field with your dad, and I think you need to help your sisters in the garden." Though Karen had seven brothers and sisters, there was always work on the farm to keep them busy.

Rebecca Peterson, age 11

But before she went to work, her mother took Karen's hands in hers and prayed, "Jesus, if You desire that any of our children be a missionary to another country someday, please help them to know Your will. Help

Karen to have a happy heart in being a little light for Jesus right now. In Jesus' Name, Amen."

She gave her mom a big hug, thanked her, and skipped off to the garden to help her sisters.

Karen continued to grow in the Lord. Missionaries came frequently to speak at their church, and her interest in missions grew as well. After graduating from high school, she attended the Lutheran Bible Institute in Minneapolis, Minnesota, for two years. She then accepted a call to serve as Parish Worker at Oak Valley Lutheran Church in Velva, North Dakota. She enjoyed working with the Sunday School, the youth, and the women's ministry, directed the junior choir, and did secretarial work in the office.

After serving at Oak Valley Lutheran Church for almost two years, Karen started feeling there was something missing. Even though she was happy in her work, she did not have a peace in her heart. For several weeks she had trouble sleeping. Then one evening Karen was reading Philippians 4:6-7: "Be anxious for nothing, but in everything by prayer and supplication with thanksgiving let your requests be made known to God. And the peace of God, which surpasses all comprehension, will guard your hearts and your minds in Christ Jesus." Karen realized she needed to talk to the Lord about the peace she was seeking. She knelt beside her bed and prayed, "Jesus forgive me for not coming to You in prayer sooner. Whatever I need to do to have this peace with You, I'll do." That evening Karen slept very well.

Two days later, something very special happened. Karen received a letter from the Mission Department of the Lutheran Bible Institute in Minneapolis, announcing a scholarship for one year of study in World Missions. Someone had recommended her for the scholarship. That evening her devotions were from Matthew 28:18-20: "Go therefore and make disciples of all the nations . . ." It was then that Karen experienced the deep joy and peace in Christ that she had been seeking.

Two months later, Karen went back to the Lutheran Bible Institute, where she spent a full year studying Missions. In February, she received a letter of call from the Evangelical Lutheran Church to serve as a missionary in Africa or Madagascar. Karen phoned her parents to tell them the news. After much prayer, she accepted the call to go to Madagascar as a Parish Worker.

The following weekend, she went home to tell her family. They were happy for her. Her mother said, "It will be a long way from home, and you will be gone a long time. But if this is your calling, we support you, and you have our blessing."

Karen's dad, Ernest, asked, "How long will you be gone?"

"I will be gone for seven years." Tears came to both of her parents. Yet they knew Karen would be supported by much prayer from the family, church, and many friends.

When Karen was commissioned in July, her home church committed to support her financially and in prayer while she was in Madagascar.

Towards the end of August, Karen's parents took her to Erskine, Minnesota, where she and another missionary left by train for New York. Then they sailed on board a beautiful ship to France. It took them seven days to cross the Atlantic Ocean. When they arrived in LeHavre, they boarded a train for Paris to study at the L'allience Fransais Language School, where they spent one year studying the French language.

Then it was time to take another long trip by ship to Madagascar. Several other missionaries who had studied in Paris were taking the same journey. When they arrived, Karen and others spent their first year studying the Malagasy language. Language study was challenging and rewarding, though there were times of frustration and loneliness. But Karen knew that her family and friends were praying for her.

Karen served in Madagascar twelve years, working with the children, youth, and women of the church. She helped the Malagasy people distribute Christian literature from a small book store and in a traveling mobile unit and made many trips out into the villages.

It was always a joy for Karen to receive letters of encouragement from loved ones and friends back home. Every week her mother wrote about family events and hometown news, closing each letter with Scripture. Often she added these deeply comforting words: "Be content in whatever state you are in . . . as you continue to be a light for Jesus. Remember, we are praying for you and your fellow missionaries and the people in Madagascar."

QUESTIONS:
1. How did Karen become interested in missions as a child?
2. What two things did Karen's mother tell her she could do in order to know whether God was calling her to go to another country as a missionary?

3. How did her parents respond when Karen told them she was going to Madagascar?
4. Who prayed for Karen while she was in Madagascar?
5. How can you be a "light" for Jesus, no matter where you are or how old you are?

Karen (Erickson) Knudsvig graduated from the Lutheran Bible Institute in Minneapolis, Minnesota, and served as a missionary to Madagsacar under the Evangelical Lutheran Church from 1961-1973. She returned to the United States in 1973, traveling with the Malagasy Lutheran Choir as an interpreter. She then accepted a call to University Lutheran Church as Parish Worker in Grand Forks, North Dakota, where she met Gerry Knudsvig. They were married in 1974. She served as Executive Secretary of the AFLC Women's Missionary Federation from 1989-1998. Gerry passed away in 2002. Karen is a member of Ny Stavanger Lutheran Church in Buxton, North Dakota.

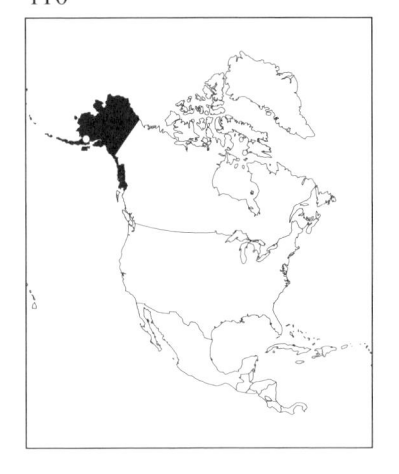

Phone Calls from God?

By Tom Olson

"Ring! Ring!"

The sound of the telephone interrupted Pastor Tom.

"Hello, Pastor Tom speaking."

"Hello. This is John Boyavich. I teach fifth grade in New Stuyahok (STOO-yah-hock). I'm bringing my class to Naknek for a field trip. We'll be using the community swimming pool but will need a place to stay overnight. Would it be possible for us to stay in your church?"

"Indeed, it would!" exclaimed Pastor Tom. "We'd love to help you out."

As soon as the arrangements were made, Pastor Tom hurried out of the office to find his wife, Sharon. He could hardly wait to tell her this exciting news. For some time they had been praying for this small village of New Stuyahok, just sixty miles away, and now it seemed that God was opening the door for them to have a definite contact.

From the time in 1997 when Pastor Tom and Sharon had first sensed God calling them to serve as missionaries in southwestern Alaska, they had experienced several miracles. "A miracle," Tom had told his three children, "is when God does impossible and unexpected things so that His will is done."

First of all, the missionary they were to replace had told Tom it would be very helpful if he would learn to fly an airplane before moving to Alaska. Villages, he had related, are not connected by roads, and small, single-engine planes are the best way to get around.

Pastor Tom had certainly never thought of flying an airplane nor did he have the necessary money to spend on learning! So they started praying for God's leading. And the miracles began! Money for the lessons came in every week from various interested people, and when Tom finished and passed his Federal Aviation Administration exam for his private pilot license, the money supply stopped as mysteriously as it had started. But another big problem loomed ahead: Where and how would he get an airplane to use in Alaska?

While reading the Bible and praying one morning, Pastor Tom had read the portion in I Corinthians 3:6-7 that God had used to call him to Alaska: "I planted," the Apostle Paul wrote, "Apollos watered, but God was causing the growth. So then neither the one who plants nor the one who waters is anything, but God who causes the growth." The Holy Spirit prompted Tom to pray specifically for a small airplane.

As he was praying, the phone rang. Rev. Paul Nash, Home Missions Director of the AFLC, greeted Tom and asked, "Tom, do you need an airplane?"

April Berntson, age 11

Stunned, Tom replied, "Paul, I was just this minute praying for one!"

"Well, my friend, God's been working that out for you before you even asked," said Paul.

Then he went on to explain how a couple from Park River, North Dakota, had felt that the Lord wanted their two-seat Cessna 150 to be used in mission work. This was another miracle from God for Pastor Tom!

And so in a short while, several skilled men were helping to rebuild the Cessna. After they had finished the work, Lavon Bohling, an experienced, certified flight instructor helped Tom fly the plane to Alaska.

After Tom and Sharon began mission work in Alaska, they soon realized just how necessary the plane was in getting from church to church since there were so few roads. In fact, this is what Pastor Tom had been thinking about when the phone call came from the schoolteacher at New Stuyahok asking if his class could stay overnight in the church in Naknek. Tom had been wondering when he would be able to go to New Stuyahok and how he could tell the people there about Jesus.

Pastor Tom's burden to bring God's love to the village of New Stuyahok had started when he met a man named Clarence. Fifty years before the Olsons came to Alaska, Clarence had attended Sunday School but then had fallen into deep sin for many years. Now he had dedicated his life to the Lord and was living for Jesus. Several weeks earlier, Clarence had come to him saying, "Pastor Tom, years ago I used to go to New Stuyahok and drink and carouse. I want so much to go back there and tell them about Jesus. Would you go with me?"

Pastor Tom had heard that the Russian Orthodox priest in New Stuyahok didn't allow evangelical ministry, and so together with Clarence, Pastor Tom and Sharon had been praying and waiting for the Lord to direct them. There was no doubt in Pastor Tom's mind that now God was opening the way for them to get to know the villagers, providing an opportunity to witness to them about Christ's love for them, and giving them a chance to show that love by offering hospitality to the students.

And now the group of sixteen fifth graders and their counselors from New Stuyahok had come by plane to Naknek, settled into the little church, and begun their grand field trip of the big town of Naknek—some five hundred people! These village kids, who spoke English heavily accented with their native tongue and interspersed their sentences with

Yupik (YOO-pick) words, were now excitedly pointing out things to one another not seen in their own village. It was so much warmer here! There were trees and bushes all around, which they did not have out on the tundra where they lived. And they marveled at all the stores where so much merchandise could be bought.

Pastor Tom wanted to call Clarence and tell him the good news about the group from New Stuyahok, but it was late. He would call in the morning. About to leave his study for the night, Tom turned out the light just as the phone rang. Who would call at this late hour? he thought to himself. Surprised, he heard the voice of Mr. Boyavich, the schoolteacher, asking if Tom could come over to the church.

"Is there anything wrong?" Pastor Tom asked.

"Oh, no, nothing is wrong. We've been having a wonderful time. But the kids have been looking at the Bibles you have here, and they are asking me so many questions that I can't answer. Will it be too much of a bother for you to come and talk to the students about the Bible?"

It didn't take Pastor Tom long to get there. Throwing on his jacket, he left the house and walked quickly to the church. The group from New Stuyahok was very curious about the Ten Commandments because they had recently seen the Disney film about Moses called "The Prince of Egypt." Pastor Tom helped them find the Commandments in Exodus 20 and spent some time telling them about God's law and sin. He had a very attentive, interested audience! Then he turned to John 3:16 and read, "For God so loved the world, that He gave His only begotten Son, that whoever believes in Him shall not perish, but have eternal life." Pastor Tom told them how Jesus had died on the cross, and that He rose again, and that they, too, could come to Him for forgiveness and salvation.

That night, seeds of God's Word were sown in the hearts of those young people! Pastor Tom realized what miracles God had performed to bring about this meeting. He remembered his own definition of a miracle: "When God does impossible and unexpected things so that His will is done." Yes, countless times God had used the ringing of the telephone to bring "good news" to Pastor Tom, and now God was using Pastor Tom to bring His Good News to Alaska!

QUESTIONS:
1. What three phone calls did Pastor Tom receive?
2. How was the first phone call an answer to Tom and Sharon's prayers?
3. Why did Pastor Tom need to learn how to fly?
4. Why did Mr. Boyavich ask Pastor Tom to come to the church?
5. What Bible verses did Pastor Tom use to help the group from New Stuyahok understand the Bible?

Pastor Tom Olson graduated from the Association Free Lutheran Theological Seminary in 1988. He served as a missionary/pilot in Alaska with his wife, Sharon, for Lutheran Mission Societies and AFLC Home Missions from 1998-2001. Sharon had previously served as a missionary in West Africa for many years. Tom has participated in the development of a Christian radio station and aviation ministry that is now reaching unreached villages and promoting increased cooperation with AFLC Home Missions in Alaska. He has also served AFLC congregations in Cloquet, Minnesota, as well as Barronett, Cumberland, and Mineral Point, Wisconsin.

The Hands That Speak

By Linda Mohagen

"It's time to go!" Henry called. Looking over his shoulder, he saw his wife hurrying toward the plane with her arms full. He had just finished the pre-flight inspection as Linda arrived with her guitar and tote bag.

"I'm so thankful for the new hangar," Henry said as he helped Linda into the plane. "It protects the plane from this bitter cold and wind."

"Oh, yes!" Linda agreed. "It's wonderful how God provided short-term mission teams from the lower states to come and help build it."

Henry buckled his seat belt before starting the engine and made certain that Linda was strapped in also. "Are you sure you have everything for the church service?" he asked.

Linda nodded in agreement. The roar of the engine swelled as they accelerated for take off. Soon they were up in the air looking down at the Alaskan frontier. They wouldn't be able to make the sixty-mile trip from Naknek northwest to the little village of Ekwok if it weren't for the airplane. Church services were held in Naknek and South Naknek on Sundays, so the Mohagens flew to Ekwok on Saturdays for services.

The airplane was climbing to altitude as Henry assured Linda, "The weather looks good for the whole trip today." Some Saturdays they hadn't been able to make the trip at all because of bad weather, and other times the ride was bumpy due to turbulence.

"It's good to see the sunshine," said Linda, relaxing into her seat. She began to think about the children she would share the Gospel with today. Linda was a ventriloquist and used puppets to tell stories from the Bible. She had learned to speak and make sounds so that her words appeared to come from a puppet's mouth. "Danny Do Little," "Sally Does Alot," and

"Memory" were some of the puppets she carried in her bag.

Looking down over the bay, Linda watched for Beluga whales, seals, and walrus. As they neared Ekwok, she spotted several moose and a large number of caribou spreading out for miles. Linda's thoughts drifted back to the first time they had flown to Ekwok. There hadn't been many in attendance at the church service there. But walking back to the plane, Henry and Linda had walked past the school where children were playing on the monkey bars. Linda was excited to see children and called out, "Hello! My name is Linda. What are your names?" She carefully listened to each name and then asked, "Do you go to church?" Not getting much response, Linda set down her guitar and took her tote bag from Henry.

"Would you like to meet my little friend?" she asked. He's a puppet, and his name is Danny Do Little.

"Yes!" they exclaimed in unison, while Linda took the puppet out of her tote. The children's faces gleamed with excitement as they came closer to see Danny Do Little. Then with no movement from Linda's mouth, Danny began telling the story of Jonah.

"Jonah was a man called by God to warn some people living in a big city to turn from their sin and to stop doing bad things."

"What bad things were they doing?" Linda asked Danny.

The puppet continued to tell the story of Jonah. Linda's excitement grew as she watched the children intent on the words that appeared to be coming from the puppet's mouth. Danny ended the story saying, "Jonah made a difference in the lives of these people. I would like to invite you to church so I can share some more stories with you that could make a difference in your life."

"Tell us more stories now!" the children shouted. They were intrigued and began to ask questions about Jonah and Jesus. Even though it was winter and the temperature was cold, they wanted to see and hear more. "Don't you have any more puppets in your bag?" they asked.

It didn't take Linda long to pull out the puppet called Memory, a very loud and excited bird. "Memory likes to learn Bible verses," Linda told the children.

"Oh, yes," shouted Memory. "I'm going to tell you one from John 3:16: 'For God so loved the world, that He gave His only begotten Son, that whoever believes in Him shall not perish, but have eternal life.' The Son that God sent is Jesus. God sent Him to save the world, which includes all of us. He came to save us from our sins. All of us were born sinners, and we do things that are not pleasing to God. But because Jesus died for our sins, we can have eternal life. God will forgive our sins when we ask Him to and will make our hearts clean."

After sharing more about Jesus, it was time for Linda and Henry to fly back to Naknek. "Be sure to come to the church when you see the plane fly in next week. We'll have lots more stories with the puppets."

On the following Saturdays that they returned to Ekwok, there were quite a few more people in church. And there were lots of children! Some of the children had brought their parents to hear Linda talk about Jesus through the puppets.

Rachel Dryburgh, age 12

Because the children weren't familiar with church services, at first they would not sit still. They walked around inside, and some even went out the door. But when Linda brought out the puppets and they began talking, the children came to the front row to listen. They also loved to sing and would sing along with the puppet, Sally. They learned songs like "Jesus Loves Me." They sang, "Jesus loves the Eskimo, Mushing dog teams through the snow. Indians and Aleuts, Wearing mukluks for their boots. Yes, Jesus loves me, . . . the Bible tells me so."

Suddenly, Linda realized that Henry was preparing to land the airplane. As the village of Ekwok came into view, Linda prayed aloud, "Thank You, Lord, for all of these memories. We pray that the seed of God's Word being planted here in Ekwok will take root and grow in the hearts of these children and their parents. We are so thankful for the privilege of teaching them." Her prayer ended with an "Amen" just as the wheels touched the ground. It was time to walk to the church and share the Good News once again through the mouths of Danny, Sally, and Memory.

QUESTIONS:
1. How did Pastor Henry and Linda get to the small village of Ekwok, which was sixty miles from their home?
2. What did Linda take along on the trip in her tote bag? Can you remember their names?
3. How did the puppets "talk"? Can you try to talk without moving your lips?
4. What Bible story did Danny share? What Bible verse did Memory recite?

Linda Mohagen is a self-taught ventriloquist and has had a puppet ministry for children for about twenty-four years. She is also an artist and substitute teacher. Her husband, Henry, has been a rancher and lay pastor. In 1999 he received his pilot's license through MATA in Arlington, Washington, and in June 2000 Henry and Linda went to Alaska where they served until October 2004. He has served churches in Rugby and Bottineau, North Dakota, and currently serves Slim Buttes Free Lutheran Church in Reva, South Dakota.

Flight Plan

By Lori Willard

It was a beautiful day to take a ferry ride across the Puget Sound from the coastland of Washington to the San Juan Islands where the AFLC Pacific Northwest District Family Bible Camp was being held. The trip would take about an hour. As friends gathered together in groups, enjoying the scenery and each other, the time passed unnoticed. When they reached the dock, everyone got back into the vehicles and after a short drive arrived at the camp. Among those in attendance were Michael Crowell, pastor of Elim Lutheran Church in Lake Stevens, Washington, and his family. The church had a very active youth group, and Pastor Crowell's teenage son, Jeremy, was one of the campers.

One of the speakers at the Bible Camp that week was a missionary who taught scriptural truths as he talked about mission work and its needs. After the evening service, the teenagers gathered around a crackling campfire. A summer ministry team from the Association Free Lutheran Bible School (AFLBS) in Minneapolis, Minnesota, led the youth in songs and devotions. One night, a team member challenged them with a pointed question: "What direction might the Lord be leading you in your life?" Through the testimonies of the team members and the biblical teaching of the missionary, fifteen-year-old Jeremy began to sense the Lord calling him into mission work.

Pondering the challenging words he had heard, Jeremy sought out his parents later that night. "Mom and Dad," he said, "as I was listening to the missionary talk about the need for missionaries around the world, the Lord laid on my heart that this is exactly what He wants me to do!" His parents were thrilled, and his mom replied, "That is tremendously exciting, son! We'll be praying for you and the Lord's direction in it all."

Soon after this experience, Jeremy went flying with his dad. Pastor Crowell had been a pilot and flight instructor for twenty years. Jeremy was fascinated with flying and always full of questions for his dad. Knowing this interest, his dad took this flight opportunity to ask, "Jeremy, have you considered mission aviation?"

Contemplating his father's question, he began to pray, "Lord, help me to know if You want me to become a missionary pilot. If You do, please open the doors necessary for me to get the training I need." His mother, Lori, who home schooled Jeremy and his sister and brother, encouraged Jeremy and prayed with him about God's will in this matter.

Together Jeremy and his dad researched mission aviation. Studying about the Civil Air Patrol (CAP), he told Jeremy, "This is an organization similar to the Boy Scouts but is based on military procedures and aviation skills." They became actively involved in CAP and soon started their own squadron in Lake Stevens. Every Monday evening was dedicated to learning more about aviation and military procedures.

In the summer months, Jeremy also attended one-week flight encampments, learning to fly an airplane. He had his first flight lesson when he was fifteen, soloed at age sixteen, and earned his private pilot's license at age seventeen. Through prayer and working together to achieve these goals, Jeremy and his dad developed a deeper relationship.

While furthering his own education, Pastor Crowell sensed the Lord leading him to begin a mission aviation training school. In October 1988, Mission Aviation Training Academy (MATA) opened, headquartered at the airport in Arlington, Washington, a short distance from the Crowell home in Lake Stevens.

As MATA developed, Jeremy worked side by side with his dad, pounding nails to build a hangar, working on the airplanes, and other endless tasks. Completing one requirement after another, Jeremy gained valuable experience working with his dad as a mechanic at MATA.

As Jeremy gained aviation experience, the sense of God's call to mission aviation continued to grow as the Lord gave him a burden for the lost. During a mission emphasis night at Elim Lutheran Church, a missionary, Pastor Dan Giles, quoted Romans 10:13-14: "For 'WHOEVER WILL CALL ON THE NAME OF THE LORD WILL BE SAVED.' How then will they call on Him in whom they have not believed? How will they believe in Him whom they have not heard? And how will they hear without a preacher?" Jeremy was especially impacted by the question, "How will they hear without a preacher?"

Emma Unverzagt, age 9

Hearing a speaker talk about a "passion for the lost" while at a Missions Fest in Vancouver, British Columbia, Jeremy's heart responded by praying, "Lord, I am willing to do whatever You would have me do and go wherever You would have me go. Give me a passion for the lost, for those who have never heard the Good News of Your Son, Jesus. Amen."

Through the tragedy of his father's death in an airplane crash in July 2005, Jeremy returned home to Lake Stevens after having spent a year studying at AFLBS. He wanted to be with his family. Bearing this sorrow, and contemplating the uncertainty of his own future, God was teaching Jeremy to rely completely on Him.

Responsible now for carrying on the work of MATA with his mother and others, he often leaned on God's promise in I Peter 4:11: "Whoever speaks, is to do so as one who is speaking the utterances of God; whoever serves is to do so as one who is serving by the strength which God supplies; so that in all things God may be glorified through Jesus Christ, to whom belongs the glory and dominion forever and ever. Amen."

Through two short-term mission trips to Naknek, Alaska, Jeremy believed God was calling him to Alaska to serve as a missionary pilot. After hearing about experiences of other missionaries from Alaska, Jeremy told his mother, "I don't feel prepared to minister to the people there. It is such a spiritually dark place. I know I need more Bible training."

This need brought Jeremy to the Association Free Lutheran Theological Seminary (AFLTS), where he continues to study as God prepares him for His Flight Plan.

QUESTIONS:
1. Through what means did God instill a desire in Jeremy's heart to become a missionary?
2. How did his parents help and encourage him in following God's call?
3. What tragedy occurred in Jeremy's life? How did it affect him?
4. Do you believe that God has a purpose for your life?
5. Are you open to God's call to serve Him, wherever that may be?

Lori (Crowell) Willard worked with her late husband, Pastor Michael Crowell, to start and maintain the Mission Aviation Training Academy in Arlington, Washington. In December 2007, Lori married Pastor Calvin Willard, who serves the Free Lutheran Church of Roseau in Roseau, Minnesota. Jeremy, a student at the Association Free Lutheran Theological Seminary, Minneapolis, Minnesota, has been on several short-term mission trips to Africa, Bolivia, Papua New Guinea, and Alaska. He is married to Lacey (Gee), a 2007 graduate of AFLBS. Lacey has also traveled on a short-term mission trip to Alaska. If the Lord wills, they plan to go as missionaries to the people of Alaska.

A Mother's Goodbye

By Ellen Monseth

The moment for departure had come. There had been much preparation and many long days and late nights of planning and packing. Every last-minute detail had been accomplished and all the lists completed.

The family was silent as they sat together, waiting until the last moment before saying that final goodbye and getting that very last glimpse of each other at the checkout counter. The plane was being readied for the long flight over the ocean, across nine time zones to the continent of Africa. It seemed so far away and so unknown. The silence served to mask their pain as tears choked out any expression in words. They were experiencing the beginnings of the pain of separation—of saying goodbye to a loved one. They were uncertain what the future would hold and even if they would see each other again in this life.

This "little girl" of Ellen's looked so young and fragile, so unaware of the challenges she would face. She did not know, nor did Ellen, what lay ahead. Mother and daughter had prayed together, talked long hours together, sought after God's heart together, and now they silently wept together. Rhoda had been "theirs" for twenty-eight years—delighting their home with her happy smiles and loving attitude. She had a tender heart for God, and following His purpose in her life had been her desire from childhood. It seemed she had always desired to care for little orphans in far off lands and tell them the story of Jesus. During her home schooling years, they had read many missionary stories together with her siblings and talked about the needs of others around the world.

"How can I withhold this child of mine and keep her to myself when You, Lord Jesus, have given Your very life for me and all mankind?"

Ellen had prayed. She was in the process of giving her daughter back to God to use in His kingdom's work. She was fearful and sad, but she was also excited and at peace. The dark and threatening "what ifs" of her mind did not overpower the faithful and comforting promises of God and His presence.

Why, Ellen wondered, is parting so difficult when I know that God is guiding? Why do tears still come when there is joy and anticipation in this new path ahead? She realized that it was moments like these that helped her to understand just a little more the greatness of her God and His love for her family and for all mankind. This wise and loving God created within her a heart for Him with a desire to please Him. This same heart, she knew, also had the capacity to dearly love and cherish those near her on this earth.

The moment for departure had come. Before her very eyes, her "little girl" with the bouncy, soft brown curls framing her face had grown to mature and beautiful, young womanhood with a loving husband and two precious children of her own. God had put within her the desire to know and do His will. God had made Himself known to her as Lord, as

Zofeyah Unverzagt, age 6

Savior, and as the all-sufficient One. He was going with her. He was going before her. She was safe in His care. Portions of II Corinthians 4, which they had recently memorized together, brought their eyes into focus that day of departure and many days after: "While we look not at the things which are seen, but at the things which are not seen; for the things which are seen are temporal, but the things which are not seen are eternal" (v.18). God was giving the family strength to persevere as they believed this truth—God calls and gives strength for the task.

As tears misted their eyes during that last goodbye, they were experiencing the grace of God in their lives, the grace which was sufficient for this very moment and for many moments thereafter. Mother and daughter had memorized II Corinthians 12:9, and now they were claiming it as their very own: "And He has said to me, 'My grace is sufficient for you, for power is perfected in weakness.'"

Though the miles are great between Ellen and Rhoda, communication is frequent because of the technologies of the day. They both remain secure in God's hands with rejoicing hearts, knowing they are being a part of His kingdom's work. Psalm 34:15 brings them comfort and strength: "The eyes of the LORD are toward the righteous and His ears are open to their cry."

QUESTIONS:
1. What does God promise to those who are willing to surrender their lives in service to Him? (II Corinthians 12:9, Philippians 4:13)
2. Why don't we need to fear what lies ahead? (Psalm 34:15)
3. Why is parting with loved ones difficult when we know God is guiding our path?
4. What is temporary in this life? What is eternal?

Ellen and her husband, Dr. Francis Monseth, along with their two youngest children, spent several months in Latvia in 1993-1994. During that time, Dr. Monseth assisted with the beginning of a Lutheran seminary in Riga, Latvia, and also taught pastoral training seminars in Estonia and Russia. Francis and Ellen have returned to Latvia, Estonia, and Russia several times on teaching missions since that time. Dr. Monseth serves as Dean of the Association Free Lutheran Theological Seminary, Minneapolis, Minnesota. They are members of Grace Free Lutheran Church, Maple Grove, Minnesota. Their youngest daughter, Rhoda, and her husband, Nathan, now serve as missionaries in Uganda, Africa.

Hail to the Brightness

Thomas Hastings
Lowell Mason

1. Hail to the bright-ness of Zi-on's glad morn-ing, Joy to the lands that in dark-ness have lain! Hush'd be the ac-cents of sor-row and mourn-ing, Zi-on in tri-umph be-gins her mild reign.

2. Hail to the bright-ness of Zi-on's glad morn-ing, Long by the proph-ets of Is-rael fore-told; Hail to the mil-lions from bond-age re-turn-ing! Gen-tiles and Jews the blest vis-ion be-hold.

3. Lo, in the des-ert rich flow-ers are spring-ing, Streams ev-er co-pious are glid-ing a-long; Loud from the moun-tain-tops ech-oes are ring-ing, Wastes rise in ver-dure and min-gle in song.

4. See, from all lands, from the isles of the o-cean, Praise to Je-ho-vah as-cend-ing on high; Fall'n are the en-gines of war and com-mo-tion, Shouts of sal-va-tion are rend-ing the sky.

South America

Quito ★
ECUADOR
• Cañar

BRAZIL

BOLIVIA
★ LaPaz

Brasilia ★

• Campo Grande

Maringa São Paulo • Rio de Janeiro
Cianorte • •
• Campo Mourão
Campo • Curitiba
Largo

Pacific Ocean

Atlantic Ocean

Snapshots

By Ruby Abel

Ruby sat quietly, teacup in hand. A slow smile spread across her face as she rested in her favorite chair with pictures spread over the table. Each snapshot brought a different memory, scenes drifting by in the afternoon sun. Was it really over fifty years since she and John had left the United States for Brazil?

The truth was evident in the photos. She picked up a faded black and white photo. How different the boys looked. They were so small, all lined up at the airport, waiting to fly to Maringa (mah-ring-AH) on their way to Cianorte (SEE-ah-NOR-tcheh) to be reunited with their father. The anticipation was evident in their smiles. David and Jonathan were beaming, and little Paul, only a month old, was in Kiyoko's (kee-YOH-koh) arms.

Kiyoko—what a blessing she had been! How wonderfully the Lord had used her. While they were in language school in São Paulo, Ruby and John had received a letter from a friend they had met in their Bible School days in Minneapolis. Their friend, Froidys, had become a missionary to Japan and had written to them: "A dear friend, Kiyoko, has moved with her family from Japan to Brazil. Her family is still Buddhist, but Kiyoko has accepted Christ and is a strong, dedicated Christian. Could you use her in your plans to begin work in the Brazilian interior?"

Ruby and John had talked it over, prayed about it, and asked the Lord to provide funds for an airline ticket for Kiyoko to join them in language school in São Paulo. Their prayers were answered, and soon Kiyoko ("Kitty," as they called her) arrived. The whole family fell in love with her from the start. Kitty could do anything from starting a fire in the brick cook stove to transferring hot coals into the charcoal iron to iron their clothes.

Elise Ackerman, age 9

Now Ruby smiled as she thought about the trip from Maringa to Cianorte in the jeep with Kiyoko and the children. John had gone ahead to begin the work, so he was familiar with the territory.

But this was the first time Ruby had seen the area they would be working in. The road was hardly passable. There were no bridges, so they had crossed the Ivai (EE-vah-ee) River on a wooden ferry that looked more like a barge. They had driven for a long time through fire that flamed up on both sides of the road. They had found out later the Brazilians were cutting down the jungle and burning the brush to clear land for planting coffee. At the time, however, it had been frightening as they drove through the walls of fire.

Ruby reached for another stack of snapshots. Here she saw Kiyoko with some children from the church. They were Japanese immigrant children that had also come to Brazil. Kiyoko was able to speak to them in their native language, and because she knew Japanese, she became the instrument God used to bring these children to hear the Word of God. Ruby thought of Isaiah 55:10-11, the verses she had so often shared with the Brazilians: "For as the rain and snow come down from heaven, and do not return there without watering the earth and making it bear and sprout, and furnishing seed to the sower and bread to the eater; so will My word be which goes forth from My mouth; it will not return to Me empty, without accomplishing what I desire."

As she set her teacup aside, Ruby thought about the great mysteries of God: How God had used their friend from Bible School, a recent missionary to Japan, to send a newly converted Japanese girl to Brazil to help them with their family. And because of this, how Kiyoko became the means by which God was able to reach the Japanese children in Cianorte.

QUESTIONS:
1. Describe the conditions John and Ruby faced when they first arrived in Brazil in the 1950s.
2. One of the benefits older Christians have is the ability to reflect over a lifetime, observing how God has led and provided for His children of all ages. Explain how this is evident in what Ruby Abel shares in this story.
3. Explain Isaiah 55:10-11 in the context of the story. Have you heard about or experienced this scriptural truth in other settings?

Ruby (Hitterdal) Abel was born in Hitterdal, Minnesota, and met John while both attended Concordia College. She attended the Lutheran Bible Institute in Minneapolis while her husband attended Luther Seminary. After seminary graduation in 1952, they went to Brazil with their young son David to serve under World Mission Prayer League. They served under WMPL from 1953-1957 and under the Evangelical Lutheran Church from 1958-1962. In 1964, she and Pastor Abel returned to Brazil and founded the first AFLC Mission in Campo Mourão, Paraná. For the next twenty-seven years, they pioneered several congregations in Brazil. Though retiring in 1991 from full-time mission work, they return annually to Brazil for evangelistic meetings.

"Snakes!"

By Ruby Abel

"Snakes! Snakes!" she whispered to herself. Ruby Abel looked out the window of her home. Her sons, David, Jonathan, and Paul, were chasing each other through the grass in the backyard. There could be snakes in that grass, she thought. And she could feel her throat tightening, ever so slightly. But then a calmness settled over her as she thought about her old fear of snakes.

Many years earlier, she and her husband, John, were preparing for full-time ministry. She was attending the Lutheran Bible Institute in Minneapolis, and he was finishing his senior year at Luther Seminary in St. Paul. After reading several articles about Brazil, she remembered how the Lord seemed to be drawing them to this developing country.

This was especially true after reading about Brazil in a 1951 *Reader's Digest* article called "Go West Young Man." It told about the great population movement from Brazil's coastline westward into the vast jungles of the hinterland. Land companies were buying up huge tracts of land, cutting roads through the jungle, and clearing tracts for new villages about every ten miles. Plans were also being made for larger cities in the future. According to the article, waves of people were moving inland to buy land to plant coffee—"Green Gold" was the name speculators were calling coffee. But there was also a great need for schools and churches on this new frontier.

In the past the Lord had been leading them to South America, but now more than ever they felt the country was Brazil.

But the more John talked about Brazil, the more Ruby's imagination ran wild with images from the jungle. The one thing she feared most was snakes! Sometimes she would imagine herself riding through the jungle on horseback with snakes hanging from trees—green snakes, blending in with the leaves, waiting for their prey to pass. She had also heard about anacondas, the enormous, thirty-foot snake that could crush a victim in a matter of minutes. And what about boa constrictors? If animals as big as cows could be crushed by them, what chance would she have?

And to make matters worse, her son David was less than a year old! What would happen to him?

Ruby often shared these fears with John. Finally, one day John said to her, "Ruby, dear, I'm really concerned about your fear of snakes. Why don't you talk to one of the professors at Bible School about this? I'm sure one of them could help you."

Ruby agreed and went to see Pastor Herman Lunder. She told him about her fear of snakes. He listened carefully. Then he asked her to open her Bible to II Timothy 1:7. He had her read out loud: " For God has not given us a spirit of fear, but of power and of love, and of a sound mind" (NKJV).

Pastor Lunder asked, "If God has not given you the spirit of fear, who has given it to you? It must be Satan." He continued, "Yes, Satan knows

Kaelyn Anderson, age 13

that with fear in your heart you may never get to the mission field." Then he prayed with Ruby, asking God to take away her fear of snakes and replace it with a spirit of trust in Him for help. He prayed that she would always remember that fear is a work of Satan, and that the Lord is greater than Satan. She then confessed her fears to God and asked Him for faith to trust Jesus for the future.

After language school they had moved five hundred miles into the jungle interior. Now as she watched her boys playing outside in the grass, running and hiding without a care in the world, and teasing each other, Ruby smiled calmly and repeated the words: "For God has not given us a spirit of fear, but of power and of love, and of a sound mind."

QUESTIONS:
1. Besides snakes in this story, what other hardships do missionaries face on the foreign field? List as many as you can.
2. For Ruby Abel, the thought of being around snakes was very upsetting. What are some other fears that people have?
3. How did Ruby learn to deal with her fears? To what degree would the advice the pastor gave her apply to others who are struggling with fear?

Ruby (Hitterdal) Abel was born in Hitterdal, Minnesota, and met John while both attended Concordia College. She attended the Lutheran Bible Institute in Minneapolis while her husband attended Luther Seminary. After seminary graduation in 1952, they went to Brazil with their young son David to serve under World Mission Prayer League. They served under WMPL from 1953-1957 and under the Evangelical Lutheran Church from 1958-1962. In 1964, she and Pastor Abel returned to Brazil and founded the first AFLC Mission in Campo Mourão, Paraná. For the next twenty-seven years, they pioneered several congregations in Brazil. Though retiring in 1991 from full-time mission work, they return annually to Brazil for evangelistic meetings.

Bruno

by John Abel

In the mid 1950s, Rev. John and Ruby Abel began their missionary work in Cianorte (SEE-ah-NOR-tcheh), a village in the Brazilian interior that had just been cut from the jungle. Even though the jungle still pressed in around the small town, an endless stream of young Brazilian families arrived day after day to settle on the small tracts of land that were becoming available for planting coffee. Not a school nor a church had been built in Cianorte when the Abels arrived, so Pastor Abel had the privilege of being the first pastor in this new town in the state of Paraná (pah-rah-NAH).

One of the first couples to come to Christ through the Abels' ministry was the recently married Francisco and Geni. They had moved to Cianorte to start a new life after Geni's father had been killed in a gun battle in another state. Rather than taking part in a never-ending blood feud with their neighbors, they decided to leave for the frontier. Only twenty-two years old at the time, Francisco was already a skilled carpenter and cabinet maker and had little trouble finding work in this fast growing frontier town. It was to his cabinet shop Pastor Abel had gone for help in making benches for their little "storefront church." Through that contact, the Abels were able to share Christ with the young couple who after a time gave their hearts to Christ and became pillars in the new congregation.

Being a fine carpenter, Francisco built his house in the style of all the other houses on the frontier. Logging was the first industry to move through the interior in the 1940s and 1950s. The loggers cut off the huge, hardwood trees three to four feet above the ground and left the stumps behind. When the settlers came, they cut off the remaining stumps at ground level, hauled them back to the village, and buried them about a foot into the ground, leaving two to three feet sticking up. Then they nailed their hardwood floors to the stumps and raised the houses.

It didn't take Francisco long before he had finished building a fine home with an extra bedroom for his brother who often stayed with them.

Built this way, the houses were well-suited for the Brazilian interior. The hardwood foundation stumps never rotted, and since the house was about three feet off the ground, the summer wind blew under the house and kept it cool. At night or when it was raining, the chickens, pigs, and dogs found shelter under the house. The space also provided a great storage area for tools and other equipment. But there was always concern that these houses built on "stumps" provided shelter for snakes, sand fleas, and other vermin.

Shortly after they moved into their new home, their chickens began making odd, squawking noises in the middle of the night. But after a few minutes, they would settle down again. Night after night this strange occurrence continued. Something was disturbing their chickens. Finally, Francisco lit his lantern and crawled under the house to take a look. In the shadows, he could see something—something bigger than a chicken! As he held up the lantern, he finally made out what it was. Huddled against his wheelbarrow was a frightened little boy!

Instead of chasing him away, Francisco reached out and took the hand of the terrified little street boy and brought him into the house. Geni made him something to eat, and they learned his name was "Bruno."

He was only six years old. His mother had died, and his father had taken a job clearing land in the jungle and left him behind. By day Bruno shined shoes and begged on the street near the bus depot. By night he looked for shelter wherever he could find it. Since Francisco and Geni did not have a dog that would chase him away, their house provided the perfect place to sleep. Careful to come after dark and leave at the first sign of morning, Bruno avoided being seen. But now having been discovered, Geni gave him a bath and made him a warm bed in the pantry.

The next Sunday they brought Bruno to church and introduced him to the congregation as the "new member" of their family. As recent converts, Francisco and Geni were putting into practice their newfound Christian love. And though Geni and Francisco were soon expecting their first child, they raised Bruno as if he were their own.

Hunter Berntson, age 8

For several years, Bruno lived with them. Francisco added another bedroom for him and taught him the skills of a carpenter. All the while he was growing up, Bruno faithfully attended Sunday School and church.

Finally, when he was a teenager, an uncle arrived, and Bruno went to live with him. But the seed had been planted in love, and although he moved away, the Holy Spirit continued to watch over him and perfect the work of salvation. In later years, Bruno returned several times to visit the missionaries.

QUESTIONS:
1. What brought people to the frontier of central Brazil at this time?
2. How did the Lord guide Pastor Abel to Francisco?
3. How did Francisco and Geni demonstrate what Christ said in Matthew 25:40: "'Truly I say to you, to the extent that you did it to . . . , even the least of them, you did it to Me'"? (Read Matthew 25:31-40)

John Abel graduated from Luther Seminary in 1952. He and his family first served as missionaries to Brazil under World Mission Prayer League from 1953-1957 and under the Evangelical Lutheran Church from 1958-1962. From 1963-1964, Pastor Abel served as the first Director of World Missions for the AFLC, and in 1964 the Abels returned to Brazil and founded the first AFLC Mission in Campo Mourão, Paraná. During a lifetime in Brazil, the Abels pioneered ten congregations and started five schools. In 1991 John and Ruby left the foreign field to accept a call as full-time evangelist for the AFLC until his retirement in 1993. Since then, he and his wife Ruby have returned annually to Brazil for evangelistic meetings. When in the United States, they reside in Hitterdal, Minnesota, where he continues to serve as an interim pastor. At present, Pastor Abel is working on a biography of his life in missions.

Nida

By Alvin Grothe

Brazil is a country of contrasts, and Campo Mourão (CAHM-poh moh-RAH-oh) is a good example of this. Carved out of the jungle, Campo Mourão was just eighteen years old in 1966, the year Missionary Alvin Grothe and his family arrived, yet the population had already reached thirty thousand. Every day the busy city was jammed with cars, trucks, bicycles, horses, and even oxcart teams. When it was dry, clouds of red dust rose from the dirt streets; when it rained, the streets became channels of mud. Main Street was the only paved street in the whole city.

Dirt roads led into the city. Dirt roads led out of this city which had grown up in the jungle some four hundred miles west and south of São Paulo, one of the world's largest cities.

Though Campo Mourão had been built by rich coffee plantation owners, most of its residents were poor, especially in Lar Paraná (LAHR pah-rah-NAH), the community on the edge of town where the Grothes lived. Their milkman, a mere boy, delivered milk from a cart drawn by a skinny horse. He would dip his ladle into the milk can and fill the containers people brought to him. The milk in the can was unpasteurized, unhomogenized, and unvitaminized!

Everyone ate beans and rice. Coffee was plentiful, but meat was not.

Houses were hastily built. Vertical boards for siding ran from the floor to the roof with small strips of boards covering the cracks between them. Often the floors were dirt, but if people could afford it, a wood floor was built, and the houses rested on wooden blocks. Most houses were not heated, and nights were often cold. It was not uncommon to see children huddled up against the outside of their house seeking warmth from the morning sun.

Pioneer missionaries Pastor John and Ruby Abel had started the work in Campo. When the Grothes arrived, the Abels were serving the Central Church at the other end of town. The Grothes began their work in Lar Paraná by starting a Sunday School class that met at the home of a widow and her young son. As the work grew, Pastor Grothe used his carpenter skills to build a small church similar to the houses in the area—dirt floor, wooden shutters, vertical siding, and a red tile roof.

One of the first couples in Lar Paraná to receive Jesus as their Savior was Sr. Pedro and his wife. Because Pedro was almost blind, their poverty was even greater than most. They lived in a small shack in the country, which was owned by the landlord Pedro worked for hoeing beans, rice, and corn. Often Pedro had no food except for tea from native leaves and grasses, so the Grothes brought him beans and rice whenever they could.

Pedro had an only daughter named Nida (NEE-dah), the saddest little girl, who never smiled. Though she was two years old, she could not walk. She had an open sore on her side that was constantly running. It was obvious she suffering from malnutrition, but there was nothing they could do since they were too poor to pay for medicine or doctor care.

All they could do was look to the Lord and pray, "Lord, help our little girl," and claim the promise in Psalm 46:1: "God is our refuge and strength, a very present help in trouble." The Grothes often joined them in prayer, asking God's guidance: "Lord, show us what we can do. Help us put feet to our prayers."

Finally, the answer came. The Lord made it clear to them that in spite of their small missionary salary, they were infinitely richer in material things than Pedro's family. Though Pedro's family had the richness of Christ in their lives, God would provide the material needs of their daughter through the Grothes.

One day the Grothes drove out to the country and asked Pedro and his wife if they wanted to leave Nida with them for a while to see if they could nurse her back to health. They agreed, so the Grothes brought her home. The Grothe children welcomed her into the family and so did their German Shepherd.

It took months of nourishing food, medication, and loving care, as well as the assistance of a doctor before improvement began to show. But God's hand was upon her, and finally, Nida began to smile, then she began to talk, and finally she could walk.

After four months, she was a healthy, normal child, and the bonds of love were growing strong between them. Nida began calling them "Momma and Daddy," and the Grothes had to make a decision.

One day they drove out to visit Pedro and his wife. With much discussion, sharing, and praying, the Lord made it clear to them that Nida should return to her parents. And so they left the smiling, happy child with her parents in their little shack in the country.

Some time later, Pedro and his family decided opportunities would be better in the little village of Santo Rei (SAHNT-oh RAY), literally the "Holy King," about fifty miles from Campo. But there was even more poverty there, and shortly after moving to Santo Rei, Nida became very sick. In desperation, Pedro tried to find some way, some means of transportation to bring her back to Campo. Finally, he got a ride with a trucker, but it was too late. Within a short time after arriving in Campo, Nida went home to be with Jesus.

Solveig Twedt, age 9

Pedro had no money for a funeral, so Pastor Grothe built the little coffin out of pine, and Mrs. Grothe and Mrs. Abel lined it with soft cloth. After a short, graveside service with some church members, the Grothes, and the Abels, Nida was buried in a red dirt cemetery reserved for the poor. The only marker on her grave was a mound of dirt and a crude cross made of sticks.

But through it all—the poverty, the blindness, the sickness, and even the death of Nida—God's grace was sufficient. Pedro and his wife went on living for the Lord, living for Jesus!

QUESTIONS:
1. How is Brazil a country of contrasts? Explain.
2. Why were Pedro and his wife so poor?
3. Why did the Grothes bring Nida back to live with her parents?
4. In what ways did the Grothe family demonstrate the love of God?

Alvin Grothe was one of the first AFLC Missionaries to Brazil, serving from 1965-1967 in the Campo Mourão area. Skilled with hammer and saw, Missionary Alvin Grothe built several churches in the short time he and his family were in Brazil, including the church in Lar Paraná that still serves our AFLC congregation there. While on medical leave in 1968, his wife Francis died. He graduated from the Association Free Lutheran Theological Seminary in 1972 and served congregations in Stacy, Minnesota, and Astoria, Oregon. Retired and living in Astoria, Oregon, he and his wife, Loretta, are members of Bethany Lutheran Church.

Promises for Dulcé

by Helen and Carol Knapp
(as told to Candice Johnson)

God had blessed Dulcé (dool-SAY) with a wonderful family. She had grown up with eight brothers and sisters. And just a few months ago, she had married a wonderful man, Paulo Fujii. Life was just wonderful for Dulcé!

Paulo, however, was becoming concerned about how he was going to provide for his new wife who was now expecting a *bebê* (bay-BAY). Good-paying jobs were hard to find in Brazil. Paulo heard the country of Japan was offering high-paying jobs to any Brazilian whose ancestors were Japanese. Many years before Paulo was born, his ancestors had left Japan and moved to Brazil. Since Paulo was Japanese-Brazilian, he qualified for one of the high-paying jobs in Japan.

Dulcé's new husband decided to accept Japan's offer and leave for a new country and a new job. But only Paulo went to Japan. Dulcé stayed in Brazil with her family. Paulo had promised he would work in Japan for only three years. During those three years, he would make enough money so he and Dulcé could live comfortably. Then he would return home to Brazil.

"Dulcé, I will come back to Brazil in three years," Paulo promised. "We will be a family again—you and I and the *bebê* you are going to have."

Paulo quickly made arrangements to leave for Japan. It wasn't long before he boarded the plane at the São Paulo airport and left Brazil.

"Being separated from Paulo for three years will be difficult," Dulcé told her father and mother and eight brothers and sisters as they all gathered together to share a meal of beans and rice. Dulcé added, "Many years ago I trusted Jesus to be the Savior and Lord of my life. Now while Paulo is gone, I will continue to trust in Jesus' promise that He will be my constant companion."

The first few months after Paulo had gone to Japan, Dulcé kept busy preparing for their *bebê* to be born. When she gave birth to a baby boy, she named him Paulo Henriqué (en-REE-kay). Now she and *bebê* Paulo Henriqué together would wait for Paulo to return.

After three long years, Paulo returned to Brazil. Dulcé, her *bebê*, and her whole family drove to the São Paulo airport to meet Paulo and celebrate his homecoming. There were plenty of hugs for everyone. Tears of joy flowed freely.

It's so wonderful to be together as a family, Dulcé thought. Paulo and me and *bebê* Paulo Henriqué! Together! *La família* (fah-MEE-lee-ah)! Thank you, God, for bringing Paulo safely home to Brazil.

But in the midst of all the hugs and tears at the airport, Paulo told everyone how much he enjoyed his job in Japan. He was making a lot of money, and he wanted to keep the job. He wanted to move his young *família* back to Japan.

How can I leave my church, Dulcé thought, and my family? My mother and father, my brothers and sisters, my Brazil! Paulo promised! He was going to go to Japan for only three years and then come home and stay with his *família*. He promised!

Dulcé looked out at all the people scurrying around the crowded São Paulo airport. People, people, *pessoas* (peh-SOH-ays)! Everywhere *pessoas*! This is how the little, island-country of Japan would be all the time—crowded with people. Paulo promised we wouldn't have to go to Japan. Now he's broken his promise.

Sad thoughts swirled in Dulcé's mind, but right now she was so thankful to have Paulo back home that she pushed these thoughts out of her mind.

Dulcé was especially excited to be able to worship together as a family at Lar Paraná Free Lutheran Church in Campo Mourão (CAHM-poh moh-RAH-oh). While Paulo was in Japan, Missionaries George and Helen Knapp and their family and all the people of the little Free Lutheran Church had become very dear friends to Dulcé. Her church family prayed for her, spent time with her, and reminded her of Jesus' promise to be her constant companion. Now that Paulo was home, she would share with her church family how thankful she was to God for bringing her little *família* together.

But soon after he arrived home, Paulo started making arrangements to take his family back to Japan. Dulcé's heart ached with the thought of moving so far away. She would miss seeing the umbrella-topped Paraná pine trees and tasting the thick, sweet, Brazilian coffee. Her heart ached the most when she thought about leaving her Brazilian *família* and her church. She already felt homesick.

Nicholas Reynolds, age 11

This feeling of homesickness reminded Dulcé of the summer when she was twelve years old and went with Missionaries George and Helen Knapp to the children's camp at *Fazenda Retiro* (fah-ZEN-dah ree-TEE-roh)—a rustic farm retreat center. She was away from her family for a whole week and had gotten homesick then too! As she thought more about children's camp, the memories of homesickness were soon replaced by much more pleasant memories. It was there she had recognized Jesus as the one and sufficient Savior of her life. These memories gave her peace.

But the thought of going to Japan was always present. She thought about all the familiar things she would miss. However, Dulcé smiled at the thought of something she would not miss—the red, Brazilian soil that stained everything, especially Paulo Henrique's white socks. She wouldn't miss all the scrubbing to clean out the red stains.

Dulcé longed to ask Pastor Knapp what she should do. He certainly would give her godly advice. But he and his family no longer lived in Brazil and had returned to the United States. So Dulcé went to her new pastor, praying that God would give him words of wisdom to share with her.

"Pastor," Dulcé pleaded, "please help me understand what God's will is for me. I want to go with Paulo to Japan, but I also want to stay in Brazil with my family."

"Dulcé, you and Paulo and *bebê* Paulo Henriqué are a new family now," explained the pastor. "God would want you to go with Paulo. He is your husband. Go! Leave your Brazilian family and go!"

From that moment on, Dulcé's doubts and fears were gone. Her aching heart was now filled with peace that only God could give.

When she arrived home again, Dulcé prayed, "Dear God, thank You for taking away my doubts and fears. Because You are everywhere, I know You are going with me and Paulo and *bebê* Paulo Henriqué to Japan. I know You will keep Your promise to be our constant companion. Even though people may break their promises, thank You that You always keep Your promises. Please lead me to a church where I can meet with other Christians."

So on August 1, 1996, Dulcé, Paulo, and *bebê* Paulo Henriqué boarded an airplane in São Paulo, Brazil, and several hours later walked off the plane in Nagoya, Japan—a new *família* in a new country.

Two weeks later, Dulcé met another Brazilian couple. "Do you know of a Christian church where I can go to worship next Sunday?" Dulcé asked.

"Yes, we go to a Christian church. You can come with us," they replied.

What joy to serve a God who keeps His promises, thought Dulcé. Just as the missionaries in Brazil told Dulcé about Jesus' love and forgiveness, she is now doing the work of a missionary in Japan, telling others of Jesus' love and forgiveness and His promise to be their constant companion.

QUESTIONS:
1. Why did Paulo go to Japan?
2. How did God help Dulcé when she thought about being homesick?
3. What things in Brazil would Dulcé miss? What one thing would she not miss?
4. What promises were made to Dulcé, and how did they turn out?

George and Helen Knapp, along with their four children, sailed for Brazil in May 1958. In 1968 they became affiliated with the AFLC, and George was ordained in 1975. They spent thirty-two years in Brazil, teaching English, serving as houseparents for missionary children, planting churches, and teaching in the Seminary and Bible School in Campo Mourão, Paraná, Brazil. They retired in 1989 and live with their daughter Carol in Willmar, Minnesota.

Precila's "Mansion"

By Connely Dyrud

"Pastor Joel," Oseias called in excitement, "we finally got word from Poema (poh-EM-ah). Joana says we must bring some blankets and clothing from the Dorcas Room and come up as soon as possible. Many are suffering from the cold." The mission had been blessed with many boxes of clothes, blankets, and quilts from faithful AFLC congregations in the United States and Canada in the early 1970s. These were stored in the Dorcas Room for just such a situation.

The winter rains had been heavy and steady for weeks—unusual for this part of Brazil. The heavy rains usually come in the summer in Brazil, especially December and January.

Pastor Joel was newly arrived in Brazil and serving a little church in Cidade Poema (see-DAH-gee poh-EM-ah), "The City of Poems." The small, rural village of Poema is located on a high hill in the high plateaus of southern Brazil. Once having arrived in the village, a visitor is quick to understand the name, because the view in all directions is breathtaking. Geographically speaking, the scene is as beautiful as a "poem." But the poverty and misfortune of the people of Poema is anything but poetic.

Because of the heavy rains, the only bridge to Campo Mourão (CAHM-poh moh-RAH-oh), where he was stationed, had been washed away, and no one had been able to get there for several weekends. Now he had finally regained telephone contact with Poema with the urgent plea from the faithful Deaconess Joana: "Please come as quickly as possible and bring quilts and clothing. The winds have blown off many roofs and the people are suffering in the cold rain."

He took a couple of seminarians and loaded the Willys Jeep Station

Wagon with boxes of clothing and blankets. The trails through the jungle were muddy and slippery, so they had put chains on all four wheels and shifted into all-wheel-drive. Going uphill, Pastor Joel had to shift into low range. Going downhill, he had to shift quickly back into high range. Coming down one hill, however, he wasn't able to shift into high quickly enough to get up enough speed to fly through a big mudhole. As a result the jeep stopped abruptly in the middle of the mud and water—all four wheels spinning, as they sank slowly in the muck. He turned off the motor and tried to open the door, but the mud was so high it blocked the door, so he crawled out the window and tumbled into the mud. Though the jeep had stopped sinking, he now was sinking. Thank the Lord! He was wearing high boots. By the time he had struggled out of the mudhole, his boots were filled, he had lost a heel, and he was mud from head to toe.

The seminarians, native to these conditions, were smarter. They watched him flailing away in the mud, climbed out the window onto the roof of the jeep, grabbed a low hanging tree vine, and swung across the mudhole to dry ground. "Why didn't you tell me you're related to Tarzan?" he shouted with a chuckle. "Next time, you get out first and show me how to survive in these conditions!"

It was afternoon, and all were hungry. They began looking for a farmer with a tractor. They had no success, but a friendly farmer with a yoke of oxen finally agreed to help. The farmer had a good laugh about the situation. Why was the missionary so muddy, and the two young Brazilians so clean? When the laughter subsided, his wife graciously prepared beans, rice, fried chicken, and eggs for them.

During the meal, a bottle filled with little peppers was passed around. Each one sprinkled a few drops of liquid on his food. Pastor Joel followed their example, but instead of just a drop or two, a little pepper also fell onto his beans. No one said anything. They all watched as he took a spoonful of beans and rice—along with the pepper. That spoonful set his mouth on fire. He tried to swallow it down quickly to ease the pain, but that only made it worse. His stomach felt like he had swallowed a blow torch. He gasped for air, and his eyes filled with tears. They tried to revive him with goat's milk, but that really didn't help. "Only passing time," they said, "will ease the pain." He had learned his lesson: Stay away from "chili peppers," at least the ones in Brazil!

Back at the mudhole, the trusty oxen pulled the jeep out, and the men paid the farmer for the lunch and the pull.

Now it was getting colder, and evening was settling in. When they finally got to the river, they were not surprised to see no sign of a bridge. Their only chance was to take a run at the river and pray for the best. They took off the fan belt so the fan wouldn't spray water over the spark plugs and kill the engine while they were in the middle of the river.

As they approached the river, they saw half a dozen men and boys fishing for their supper in the swollen river. The fishermen had had no success catching fish that day, but maybe they could guide them successfully across the river. One man said, "Look, you have to go straight from here, so many meters," he pointed out over the water, "and then you have to veer to the right. If you don't, you'll crash into a bunch of rocks and then into a deep hole." He looked at Pastor Joel and saw a very bewildered man standing there. Finally, he motioned, "Come on, I'll just walk ahead of you, and you follow."

"You start praying," Pastor Joel told the seminarians who got out and walked behind the jeep, "I have to concentrate on the driving." As the river guide and his son started down into the river, Pastor Joel shifted the jeep into low range and slowly rolled into the water, sinking deeper and deeper while the water gushed up around his feet. The guide walked slowly and carefully. As the water rose past his hips, he looked straight ahead, eyes fixed on a point on the other side of the river. The jeep began to feel light. It seemed to float downstream ever so slightly as the wheels lost contact from time to time in the swift side-current.

As the man started rising slowly out of the water, they all shouted, "Thanks be to God!" Finally, the jeep grabbed solid ground. Safely out of the river, Pastor Joel opened the doors, and the water rushed out of the cab. He then switched the motor off, so it wouldn't overheat until they had the fan belt back on. But even though he had turned off the key, they could still hear the sound of a motor running. In front of the jeep, the boy was laughing and pointing. A good-sized fish was caught between the license plate and the bumper, his tail flapping against the bumper making the sound of a knocking engine. Pastor Joel grabbed the fish and gave it to the luckless guide who had caught nothing all day. At least now he would have supper.

The group finally arrived in Cidade Poema in the cold of the night. The flickering light of the kerosene lamp shown on the happy faces of Joana and her husband, Tiago, and their five children. A supper of beans, rice, fried eggs, and pork was waiting for them. How good it tasted, and finally the flame of the noontime chili was extinguished in Pastor Joel's stomach. That night they had a sweet time of fellowship—Bible reading, sharing, and praying.

As Pastor Joel lay down to sleep, all he could say was "Thank You, Jesus. Thank You, Jesus, for Your kind protection today."

Jorgie Rassi, age 7

The next day was filled with visits, Bible reading, prayer, and distribution of clothing and blankets. The last home they visited was a bleak, little shack belonging to an old widow named Precila, who was suffering from bronchitis and growing steadily weaker. She was unable to get out of her bed to make them coffee. But in her sickness and sadness, she poured out her heart.

When she and her husband were first married, they had wanted four girls and four boys, but God had not allowed them to have any children. "Our second wish," she said, "was to have a nice house on a green hill with lots of flowers. We worked, saved our money, and built our dream home on that hill up there." She pointed to a place scarcely visible in the gloomy mist. "But three years later, a fire broke out while we were working in the field. Both of us ran home to put it out, but it was too far gone. As we fought the flames, my husband slumped to the ground, never to rise again. He had suffered a heart attack and died right there."

She turned to him, shivering in the damp cold evening, and continued, "I tried to get help to put up this little shack, but no one had time to help me. It's cold, the wind and rain blow through the cracks, and I've been so cold lately."

Pastor Joel shared John 14:1-6 with her. "In My Father's house are many mansions . . . . I go to prepare a place for you" (KJV).

"Is that really true?" she asked.

"Yes," he said, "look at verse six. Christ said, 'I am the way, the truth, and the life.' Accept Christ now, and you will have a mansion in heaven."

"But can it be as nice as the one we built up there on the hill?"

"Yes, only much nicer!"

The woman cried as Joana put her arms around her and prayed with her as she received Christ that evening. Before leaving, Joana wrapped her in one of the warm quilts and left extra clothes for her.

The following week word came from Joana. They had found the little widow Precila the next day. She was covered from head to foot with the new quilt. When they pulled it back, they found her with hands folded and a smile on her face.

She was at home, happy in her new mansion that would never burn down.

QUESTIONS:
1. What problems besides language differences do missionaries face in other countries?
2. Why had Precila not been able to enjoy her earthly "mansion"?
3. Precila finally reached her heavenly mansion. List the chain of events leading to her conversion that may seem to the casual reader pure chance, but from a spiritual point of view are linked together under God's miraculous guidance.

Connely Dyrud, the "Pastor Joel" in this story, graduated from the Association Free Lutheran Theological Seminary in 1969, and he and his wife, Carolyn, left immediately for the AFLC Mission Field in Brazil. For the next thirty-five years, they served largely in the Campo Mourão area in the State of Paraná where he was Dean of the AFLC Bible School and Theological Seminary for several years. In 1991, he and Carolyn founded the Miriam Infant Home in Campo Mourão. Today, Pastor Dyrud serves as AFLC Missionary at Large and teaches part-time at the AFLC Schools. Carolyn passed away in 2005. He is a member of Grace Free Lutheran Church in Maple Grove, Minnesota.

"Why Was I Born Here?"

By Connely Dyrud

Thump! Thump! Thump! Pastor Joel's head snapped up from his chest. He had been dozing and couldn't see anyone in the darkness. Thump! Thump! Thump! On the windshield again. No wonder he couldn't see anyone—the car windows were all steamed over. He had been waiting in the car in the cold winter rain since 5:00 A.M. at the Campo Mourão (CAHM-poh moh-RAH-oh) bus depot with the heater on and the motor running.

Now he braced himself for the good-natured teasing that would come when the missionary he was waiting for had found him sleeping. "Ha! Asleep on the job, Pastor Joel!"

He quickly rolled down the window, and to his surprise it was not the smiling missionary he had expected, but a man he had never seen before. He was soaking wet, and his rough, calloused hand reached into the car, shaking in the cold. "I need money for food," he whispered.

Pastor Joel's first thought was a common reaction to beggars . . . begging for food, but all too often the money was spent on drink or drugs. Instead of reaching into his pocket, he reached into his Bible and pulled out a tract. "Here. The Lord Jesus Christ is the Bread of Life."

The man looked at Pastor Joel strangely. "I'm hungry, I can't eat paper!"

"No," Pastor Joel said, "read what the tract says about Jesus. He is the one who wants to save you!"

He put his head down and muttered, "I . . . I can't read."

Pastor Joel opened the car door and stepped out. The man was barefoot in the rain. He had no coat, only a short-sleeved, ragged shirt. He was shaking uncontrollably in the cold, July rain.

Kayla Belinski, age 14

"Could you please buy me some hot coffee and bread? I'm so cold and hungry."

They walked over to the luncheonette, out of the rain. The buses were starting to come in, but not the one from Curitiba. There would be time. Pastor Joel asked him why he was out of work. He shook his head, "No, I have work." Then, cupping his hands around the warm coffee, he began.

"My parents were farmers in Yugoslavia. They lost everything in World War II. Their home, their land, everything. Shiploads of my fellow countrymen were sent to other countries. They were called 'Displaced Persons.' Some were sent to Canada, some to America, some to Argentina, and some to Brazil. My parents were sent here to Brazil.

"As soon as they arrived, they were told about the great free land in the middle of the state of Paraná (pah-rah-NAH). It was the late 1940s and early 1950s, and this part of the country was just getting settled.

"So into the jungles my parents went. They had never experienced the heat or the rains like they found here, but both my mother and dad worked hard at clearing the jungle. All they had were axes. Everything was done by hand. They were happy because the Brazilian government gave each settler ten alquires (about sixty acres) of free land.

All I remember from the time I could walk was hard work. My sisters, my parents—all of us—fought the bugs and snakes and cleared the land, a piece at a time.

"When I was ten, my dad was bitten by a poisonous snake while he was cutting tall grass. There was no hospital, no doctor around. No one knew what to do, and so he lay screaming for almost a day before he died.

"My mother was pregnant at the time of his death, but we all worked harder to make up for the loss of Dad.

"When my mother was in labor, complications set in. There was no midwife, no one to help but us children. The baby was born dead. Then we stood by helplessly, watching mother die in agony. Then we were all alone. The next day I took my two sisters, and we tried to find our closest neighbor in the dense jungle. I was the oldest, but I could not remember where to go. So we wandered around for three days in the heat before we were finally found, half dead.

"We lived with the family that found us. The nearest school was thirty miles away, so we never got an education.

"I got married at eighteen and started raising a family of my own on five acres of land. We have some pigs and chickens, and I plant beans and rice and corn. The little money I earn goes to pay the drugstore because my daughter is very sickly."

The man was crying now as he cupped the coffee cup in his hands and brought it up to his chest for warmth.

He continued between sobs. "I rode the bus into Campo yesterday, but the price of the medicine had gone up so much I had no money left for a room or food. Last night I tried to sleep in the street, but it started raining, and I have been walking around trying to keep warm."

Pastor Joel had been silently listening to the story. Now his story told, the man was silent also. Then he turned to Pastor Joel, his blue eyes glazed with tears, and looked straight into his face. "You are not Brazilian either, are you?"

"No," the pastor agreed, "no, I am an American. My grandparents also came from Europe. I, too, grew up on a farm in the United States."

The man shook his head. "But that's not fair!" he blurted out. "Why were you born in America, and I was born in Brazil? Both our ancestors came from Europe, and look what happened to my parents and to me!"

As Pastor Joel put his arm around him, the man leaned closer, shivering and sobbing softly. Pastor Joel said, "I cannot say why I was born in one place of this world and you in another, but God our Father is near today. He never left you nor abandoned you even if your earthly father and mother were taken from you when you were so young. God was always with you, and today He wants to save you and give you a much better life."

That morning, while the buses were running late because of the heavy rains, Sr. Jose gave his heart and life to Jesus.

The bus Pastor Joel was waiting for was still delayed. Before his new friend's bus left, he gave him his sweater and some extra money. The man climbed into the bus with a smile on his face. He now had hope and a future. He was going home to Mambore, (mum-boh-RAY) a small town some miles away. Pastor Joel wondered what his chances were of continuing in the faith? He did not know. He had encouraged him to find a Protestant church in his town, though he doubted there was one. Pastor Joel had assured him that he would continue praying for him, and he left him in God's care.

As the bus slipped away in the morning dawn, Pastor Joel couldn't help but think of his question again, "Why was I born here, and you there?" Why, thought Pastor Joel, was I born in a Christian home when so many are not? Then the words of Isaiah 55:8 came to him: "'For My thoughts are not your thoughts, nor are your ways My ways,' declares the LORD."

As he sat once again in his car waiting for the bus from Curitiba, the raindrops drumming harder on the roof, he thought of what a great responsibility America has according to Luke 12:48. "From everyone who has been given much, much will be required; and to whom they entrusted much, of him they will ask all the more."

QUESTIONS:
1. Look at a globe and point to the country, state, and city where you were born.
2. Why do you think God put you in that place?
3. What can you do to help others find Jesus?

Connely Dyrud, the "Pastor Joel" in this story, graduated from the Association Free Lutheran Theological Seminary in 1969, and he and his wife, Carolyn, left immediately for the AFLC Mission Field in Brazil. For the next thirty-five years, they served largely in the Campo Mourão area in the State of Paraná where he was Dean of the AFLC Bible School and Theological Seminary for several years. In 1991, he and Carolyn founded the Miriam Infant Home in Campo Mourão. Today, Pastor Dyrud serves as AFLC Missionary at Large and teaches part-time at the AFLC Schools. Carolyn passed away in 2005. He is a member of Grace Free Lutheran Church in Maple Grove, Minnesota.

Under the Southern Cross

By Loiell Dyrud

It was fall in southern Brazil. The nights were getting cool. May had just begun, and sometimes the temperature went down to 50 degrees Fahrenheit. By July some nights might even drop to freezing, and some mornings Rafael would wake up to find a thin sheet of ice on the wooden water tub outside his back door.

The nights, too, were getting longer, and the stars in the Southern Hemisphere seemed brighter. From his bedroom window, he could see the "Southern Cross," a pattern of stars that make the shape of a cross leaning gently on its side.

Rafael (HAH-fay-el) was five years old and lived with his parents, Hosne and Marie, on the edge of Campo Mourão (CAHM-poh moh-RAH-oh). "Campo," as the locals liked to call it, was a frontier city in the high planes agricultural region in the state of Paraná. Organized a mere fifty years ago, Campo Mourão's population today has grown to more than 80,000.

Rafael's parents had gone to the Central Church in Campo Mourão for several years, and his father was taking night classes at the AFLC Bible School.

Sunday Evening Worship Services were Rafael's favorite. It is a tradition in many Brazilian churches to have Sunday School in the morning and Worship Service in the evening. Rafael liked to sit close to the front of the church, so he could hear every word. Though he was too young to read, Rafael would sit with his Bible open, following the text with his pointer finger. Sometimes Pastor Joel would be reading from John, while Rafael would have his Bible open to

Psalms. It didn't matter; he felt he was "reading" the Bible anyway.

On the way home from church, Rafael was a torrent of questions. "What does it mean to be saved?" "Where is heaven?" "Who goes to heaven?" "What are sins?" "Why did Jesus have to die?" "If I die, will I go to heaven?" Each week his parents tried their best to answer his questions. Each week they would be met with new questions and comments

Cassie Haglin, age 14

on the sermon. Often Rafael would repeat statements Pastor Joel had made in the service and ask for more explanations.

During the rest of the week, Rafael's days were spent like most children in Brazil. Playing "futbol" (soccer) in his back yard with his friend

Claudio was the most fun. Most Brazilians don't like to mow lawns, so every blade of grass and every plant is pulled out, leaving a yard of hard, red clay, perfect for soccer! The red dust rose during their frantic games as they used two stones at either end of the yard for goalposts. Some day, they were certain, they would play for Team Brazil. Some day they might even help win the Gold Cup. Sometimes Rafael pretended he was Pele, sometimes Ronaldo. Sometimes the ball went into the narrow alley and bounced among the bright red poinsettia flowers that bloomed everywhere in the fall. Often the ball went into the neighbor yards.

Across the alley lived Terezinha (ter-ah-ZIN-yah), an old woman who limped. "Stay away from her," his mother had warned. "She lives alone and doesn't like kids bothering her." Terezinha once scolded Rafael sharply when his ball had landed in her garden breaking off one of her tomato plants. But for the last two weeks, he had not seen her in the garden. Instead, a strange woman went in and out of her house several times a day.

"That's her daughter," Marie told Rafael. "Terezinha is sick, and her daughter is worried because she is so old."

One day when Marie was washing dishes, she looked out the window above her sink, and to her amazement she saw a smiling Rafael leaving Terezinha's house. He was skipping along the path, his curly, black hair bouncing. Marie was upset. Wiping her hands on her dress, she rushed out and grabbed Rafael by the arm. "Haven't I told you to stay away from her house? She doesn't want to be bothered!"

"No, Mom," Rafael pleaded, "I've been in her house many times since she got sick. She wants me to come. She says I make her happy."

"How can that be! You stay here, and I'll go over and apologize for bothering her."

Marie hurried across the alley, knocked on the door, and waited with dread. They had been neighbors for some time, yet they hardly knew each other. To the neighbors, Terezinha was considered a sharp-tongued, haughty woman, who didn't like the noise of the neighborhood, especially children, and kept to herself.

Finally, she heard a feeble "Come in." Slowly, Marie walked in and waited until her eyes adjusted to the dim light of the little one-room house. Her house was stuffy. The bare electric wires ran along the open ceiling rafters attached to glass insulators. The windows were shut, and a wood fire was burning in the small stove.

Terezinha was lying on a bed in the corner of the room. Her cheeks were hollow, and her uncombed, stringy hair was spread out like a silver fan on the dirty pillow. A wrinkled sheet covered her thin body. Gradually, Terezinha opened her dark eyes and turned to Marie. "I'm so sorry, Terezinha. I didn't know Rafael was coming here bothering you, especially when you're not feeling well," Marie offered.

Terezinha softly protested. "No, that's all right. I like when Rafael comes to see me. He's so sweet. He puts his little hand on my forehead and prays for me. And then he talks about Jesus. He tells me what the pastor says."

Marie didn't know what to say. "I, I, I'm sorry, but if it's ok with you, I, I guess it's ok with me. Should I let him come again?"

"Oh, please do. Anytime."

Marie turned to leave and then turned back again. "Is there anything I could bring you? Food or something?"

"No, my daughter looks after me. I'm ok."

As Marie walked back across the alley to her house, she whispered prayerfully, "Oh, God, how can this be? My little Rafael?"

When she got to the house, Rafael was waiting for her. "How is she, mom? She really looks tired, doesn't she?"

Kneeling down to him, Marie hugged him. "Terezinha says she likes when you come to visit her. So, I guess you can go over there again."

Two days later when Marie came back from the Bible bookstore where she worked, she saw a small group of people gathered around Terezinha's house. When she got to the yard, she heard sobbing inside and went up to a man standing by the door. "Terezinha died last night," was all he said.

Later that afternoon, when Rafael came home from his grandma's, Marie got up the courage to tell him. "Rafael, have you heard? Terezinha died last night."

"Oh, it's alright, mom. Yesterday, when I was talking with her, I said, 'Terezinha, if you died, would you go to heaven?' She said, 'No.' I asked her if she wanted to go to heaven, and she said, 'Yes.' Then I told her she could go to heaven if she would let Jesus into her heart. But she told me she didn't know how. So I told her that was ok, and I told her to say the words after me, and I told her as many of the words I could remember that I had heard Pastor Joel say—that she should ask Jesus to forgive her for her sins and that she should ask Him to come into her heart." Rafael was smiling, "And, Mom, she prayed with me. So she's ok. I'm sure she's in heaven."

Marie sat down. She reached out and hugged him and started to cry. "And, Mom," Rafael said as he squirmed free, "when I get big, I want to be a pastor, too. Is that all right?"

"Yes, Rafael. Yes, yes, yes, that's all right! But remember, Jesus can use His children of any size, of any age! You don't have to wait until you're 'big.'" She hugged him again and again. Picking him up, she rocked him in her arms from side to side.

That night when Rafael went to bed, he looked out his bedroom window and saw the Southern Cross in the cool, May night. Somehow, the Cross seemed brighter than he had ever seen it before. Then he closed his eyes and said his prayers.

QUESTIONS:
1. Why didn't Rafael use his Bible when he went to visit Terezinha?
2. When is it too late for Jesus to save a person?
3. Who helped Rafael say the right words to Terezinha?
4. What did Rafael's mother mean when she said, "Jesus can use His children of any size, of any age"?

Loiell Dyrud is a retired English teacher living in Thief River Falls, Minnesota. In 2000 and again in 2003, he visited the AFLC Mission in Brazil, spending most of the time in the Campo Mourão area with his brother, Missionary Connely Dyrud. This experience provided the background for "Rafael." He serves on the AFLC Board of Publications and Parish Education and is a member of Our Saviour's Lutheran Church in Thief River Falls.

A Fisher of Men

By Becky Abel

"I want to tell you a true story this morning," said Becky Abel as she began speaking to the Sunday School class.

"Do you remember when Jesus was walking one day by the Sea of Galilee, and He saw two brothers throwing their fishing nets into the sea, hoping to fill them with fish? He called out to them, 'Follow Me, and I will make you fishers of men.' That story is found in Matthew 4:18-19 when Peter and Andrew became disciples of Jesus. Fishing for fish was good. It was how these brothers made money to live. But Jesus had something more exciting and more important in mind for them than fishing in the lake. He wanted them to walk with Him, get to know Him, and understand that He was Messiah, the One who would save all people from sin. He also wanted them to tell everyone else about Him!"

Then Becky told the children about a little girl named Analis. Analis was only five years old when she began coming to Vacation Bible School at the ARCA Bible Camp (The Association Retreat Center in Brazil). Someone had invited her, and pretty soon she was taking part in Bible Club and Sunday School every week. How she loved being in church with the other children, singing the songs, and listening to the Bible stories! Soon she asked Jesus into her heart and asked to be baptized.

This was all a wonderful miracle, for you see, Analis was not raised in a Christian home. Her mother and father separated, and there were many problems within the family that hurt Analis. But as a young girl, Analis purposed in her heart to follow God's will for her life. She found a family and a home in a church where she was loved and where others helped her to learn more about the Lord. Missionaries Becky and her husband, Paul, became her godparents at her baptism. They encouraged Analis to keep looking to Jesus in His Word through difficult times and to be a fisher of men like Peter and Andrew. Analis grew to love the Lord more and more and loved to serve Him by singing at church and visiting those who were sick.

As young as she was, Analis started being a missionary. She invited two neighbor girls, Amanda and Ednay, to come to Vacation Bible School. These two sisters received Jesus as their Savior, too, and soon the three girls started coming to church together. The two sisters kept praying and kept inviting their mother, Cleci (clay-SEE), until she decided to come to church. Cleci had been a very bitter, unhappy woman, but when she experienced the love of Jesus, she became a new person in Christ just like it says in II Corinthians 5:17: "Therefore if anyone is in Christ, he is a new creature; the old things passed away; behold, new things have come." That means when someone becomes a Christian he becomes a brand new person inside. He's not the same anymore because a new life has begun! That's what happened to Cleci; she wasn't bitter and unhappy anymore.

Cleci, Amanda, and Ednay, along with Analis, regularly attended church together and together prayed for the conversion of Cleci's husband, Edgar. Edgar was a heavy drinker and for years and years had resisted the idea of church. He probably thought it was all right for his wife and children but not for him. But his family was praying! They knew that the Lord could help him.

Then one day, José, the local blacksmith, invited Edgar to church. José had become a Christian and wanted Edgar to experience the same joy. Edgar accepted the invitation to go to church, and in time he also became a Christian. Today Edgar is a leader in his church, and he and his family's lives are beautifully united around the cross of Christ.

Now Becky asked the Sunday School class, "Do you see the way God worked in this town? It was like a chain reaction. Someone invited Analis to VBS, she invited her girlfriends to VBS, they invited their mother to church, and they all prayed for Edgar until he became a Christian too."

A Fisher of Men

Yes, even as a little girl, Analis started being a missionary. When she grew older, she became a wonderful storyteller and served as a Bible Camp counselor and Sunday School teacher. By being obedient and following Jesus, Analis has led other children to Him.

Many times Analis has felt lonely and disappointed because even though she has many friends who are Christians, her own family does not share her life of faith. She has gone through many trials and difficulties, but God has helped her through them all and kept her faithful to Him. Analis prays for her family every day and believes that the Lord will speak to them. Maybe the Lord will use her as a "fisher of men" to lead them to Christ!

Becky stopped for a moment, gazing out over the room full of children and youth. Looking into the attentive faces, she asked, "How did you come to know Jesus? Have you ever invited someone to come to Vacation Bible School or church with you? Wouldn't you also like to be a fisher of men for the Lord? Think about Analis, and ask God what He wants you to do."

Jacob Berntson, age 9

QUESTIONS:
1. How did Analis start going to the ARCA?
2. What did she find at the ARCA?
3. How did Analis start being a missionary or a "fisher of men"?
4. How can you be a "fisher of men"?

Becky Abel is a pastor's daughter who received her call to missions at a missionary conference when she was eighteen years old. She met her husband, Paul, at Concordia College in Moorhead, Minnesota, and graduated in 1978 with a degree in Elementary Education. She and her husband have served as church-planting missionaries with the AFLC in Brazil since 1985. Besides starting churches, the Abels are directors of the ARCA Bible Camp ministry near Curitiba, Paraná, Brazil. Paul is the son of Pastor John and Ruby Abel, AFLC Missionaries to Brazil.

Freedom from Bondage

By Becky Abel

"Pastor, I have a friend who I am very concerned about," said Jaime as he and Pastor Paul Abel were leaving the church. "Would you be willing to visit him and his family?"

"Of course, Jaime. But first tell me about him and why you are concerned."

"His name is Antonio," replied Jaime. "He and Uildes (WHEEL-dees) are not married but have been living together for several years. Now they have a little baby. Shouldn't the baby be baptized?"

Pastor Paul sensed that there was more to the situation than the baby's baptism. "What else is going on in this family?" he asked Antonio.

"Well, I'm actually not sure, Pastor," Jaime replied. "But they don't know the Lord, and I think a visit would really help. Maybe it would even bring them to church."

Pondering how he should approach the situation and wanting to take advantage of the opportunity to tell this couple about Jesus, Pastor Paul arranged the visit with Uildes and Antonio.

Before leaving the house for the visit, Paul and his wife, Becky, prayed together, asking the Lord to go before him and open the hearts of Antonio and Uildes: "Lord, in Your Word You have shown us that if we need wisdom in any situation, we can come to You and ask, and You will give all that is needed (James 1:5). Together we ask for Your blessing on this meeting and that You would help us to understand the needs of this family. We pray that they will hear Your Word and open their hearts to You. In Jesus' name we pray. Amen."

Arriving at the house, Pastor Paul met Antonio and Uildes and several relatives. What a joy it was to tell them about God's love for each one of them. He explained that because of every man's sin and inability to live a perfect life, Jesus had shed His blood on the cross. He showed them this truth in John 3:16, "For God so loved the world, that He gave His only begotten Son, that whoever believes in Him shall not perish, but have eternal life." Then turning to I John 1:9, he read, "If we confess our sins, He is faithful and righteous to forgive us our sins and to cleanse us from all unrighteousness."

Pastor Paul also talked with them about baptism and what it means. He shared about the promises parents make to God when bringing their child to Him in baptism and the blessings of living according to God's plan. That evening Pastor Paul had the privilege as God's servant of leading this family to new life in Christ.

In the following weeks, the family attended Bible studies and learned about living for Jesus. The Abels and the other church members were faithful in helping and teaching them.

Through these Bible studies, the Lord spoke to Antonio and Uildes regarding their long-time addiction to cigarette smoking. They found deliverance in Jesus' name. In the studies, Pastor Paul explained about idolatry and letting Jesus have complete allegiance, showing them in Exodus 20:3 God's command, "You shall have no other gods before Me."

Neither Antonio nor Uildes had had any previous contact with Christianity. In fact, Uildes had been a practicing "spiritist," one who calls up spirits of the dead to communicate with the living at meetings called "séances." Many in Brazil practice various kinds of "voodoo," or Satan worship. Antonio's mother, also, had been a fortuneteller. But now as they continued in the Bible studies, they saw that Jesus wanted them to be free! And they wanted to be free from their sins of the past.

As time went on, Uildes became troubled about the little statue she had hidden in her bedroom. Throughout her life she had been taught to hold in reverence a statue of the Black Mary. Like most Brazilian Catholics, she believed that bad luck would come if she got rid of it. One day, convicted by the Holy Spirit that the Lord did not have her full allegiance and convinced that He was powerful enough to protect her from all harm, Uildes broke the little statue into small pieces and threw them away. What freedom she found! From that moment on, Uildes experienced true freedom from bondage to Satan—freedom through the power of Jesus Christ.

Elijah Haug, age 17

Wanting to live according to God's Word, Uildes and Antonio were married, and Antonio, who had not been baptized before, was baptized at the same time as their little son, Thomaz. The couple continued to grow in Christ and became leaders in the congregation in Curitiba. Today they have two grown children who also love Jesus and are active in the church. Uildes has been the head cook at the ARCA Bible Camp (The Association Retreat Center in Brazil) for years and blesses many with her sweet spirit and wise counsel. Over the years she has been able to help others who are bound in spiritism and idol worship. Uildes shows discernment and wisdom in counseling them and gladly shares her testimony, eager that others find the freedom that she has found in Christ.

QUESTIONS:
1. Why was Jaime concerned about Antonio and Uildes?
2. What kind of activities had Uildes been involved in?
3. How did Pastor Paul help Antonio and Uildes?
4. What idol did Uildes keep hidden in her bedroom? What did she do with it?
5. What does God's Word say about idols?

Becky Abel is a pastor's daughter who received her call to missions at a missionary conference when she was eighteen years old. She met her husband, Paul, at Concordia College in Moorhead, Minnesota, and graduated in 1978 with a degree in Elementary Education. She and her husband have served as church-planting missionaries with the AFLC in Brazil since 1985. Besides starting churches, the Abels are directors of the ARCA Bible Camp ministry near Curitiba, Paraná, Brazil. Paul is the son of Pastor John and Ruby Abel, AFLC Missionaries to Brazil.

Fighting Willy

By Jonathan Abel

Little Lara was at home in the yard when she heard the sound of fighting coming from the nearby neighborhood soccer field. Oh no, she thought, I hope Willy is not involved this time! Worried about her older brother, Lara ran as fast as she could, making her way through the crowd of chanting boys to see who was fighting. Sure enough, there was Willy rolling in the red dust with another boy. Both were struggling to get the better of the other.

Hurriedly, Lara pulled away from the crowd and ran back home, shouting, "Mommy, Mommy, come quickly. Willy is in another fight!"

Filipa came running out of the house, intent on defending her boy from anyone who wanted to hurt him. But once again someone else had gotten into trouble for a fight that Willy had started.

Actually, Willy was a good boy, but the circumstances of his family life had caused him to be rebellious. His father, an alcoholic, didn't take any responsibility in their home. And Willy and Lara never knew what he would be like when he came home, so they both tried to stay out of his way.

The children's mother was a very hard-working woman who wanted desperately to keep her family together. To do that, she worked long hours every day. Before Willy had been old enough to start school, Filipa had to leave him and Lara at home by themselves while she was at work. Afraid for the children's safety and not making enough money for daycare or a sitter, Filipa would lock the door behind her early in the morning, so the children couldn't go out in the street. She would leave them some cookies for a snack, and a neighbor would come in at noon to check on them and give them lunch. Then once again they'd be locked in until their mother arrived home in the evening. This grieved Filipa greatly, but it was the best solution she could find.

Things changed a little when Willy started school. He no longer had to stay in the house but could go out in the yard to play after school. Like all the houses in the neighborhood, theirs had a high fence around the yard, but Willy soon found a way to get over it and join his friends at the soccer field. That's when the fights began.

Perhaps it had something to do with what was going on at home. Hearing his mother and father fighting made him worried and upset, so he did everything he could to make them happy. When they divorced, he thought that it must be his fault and that he had failed. Blaming himself, he struck out at everyone for any reason.

It was at this time that missionary pastors Jonathan Abel and his father John Abel set up a large tent in Willy's neighborhood in Campo Grande, Brazil, to have evangelistic services. Willy went one evening with his mother and sister. Together the three of them responded to Pastor John Abel's invitation to receive Jesus as their Savior. It was the beginning of a new life for each of them. They became active in the Free Lutheran congregation, taking part in Sunday School, Bible studies, and helping wherever there was a need.

April Abel, age 16

Hearing God's Word on a regular basis, Willy became more and more convicted about his temper. He knew that God was not pleased when he got angry. Most of the fights Willy got into were caused by someone cheating or trying to hurt someone else, and he was determined not to let that happen. But the Lord showed Willy that this way of solving problems was not right and that his fighting was ruining his reputation in the neighborhood.

"Willy," said Pastor Jonathan, "all of this fighting is not good. It doesn't glorify God."

"I know," Willy responded, "but I just can't stand it when the boys don't play the games fairly and are always cheating."

"Remember what the Bible says: '"Vengeance is Mine, I will repay,' says the Lord" (Romans 12:19). That means that God doesn't want you to try to take care of His business! The Scripture also says, 'An angry man stirs up strife, and a hot-tempered man abounds in transgression' (Proverbs 29:22). Another verse in Proverbs says, 'Do not associate with a man given to anger; or go with a hot-tempered man, or you will learn his ways and find a snare for yourself' (Proverbs 22:24-25)."

"Willy," Pastor Jonathan continued, "is that what you want?"

"No," Willy replied. "No, I really want to change!" So together he and Pastor Jonathan prayed for God's help.

It wasn't easy to quit fighting. But now every time Willy was tempted to put up his fists and fight another kid, big or small, the Spirit would whisper these verses in his heart, and Willy would respond, letting the Lord take care of the problem His way.

The neighborhood soon recognized Willy as a very responsible young man who loved the Lord. In church he became a leader of the youth group, a Sunday School teacher, and treasurer of the congregation. Other churches in the area came to respect him as a man with a strong Christian witness. God did a great work in this young man, who chose to fight sin with the help of the Lord.

QUESTIONS:
1. What made Willy angry?
2. How did Pastor Jonathan help Willy?
3. Are there things that make you angry? Explain.
4. How can the verses in the story help you to deal with your anger?

Pastor Jonathan Abel was born in LaPaz, Bolivia, as his missionary parents were enroute to Brazil. He grew up in Parana, Brazil, but his last high school years were spent in the United States. He graduated from Moorhead State University. He attended AFLBS and graduated from the Lutheran Brethren Seminary, Fergus Falls, Minnesota. Throughout his years of schooling in the United States, he returned to Brazil for short periods. He met his wife, Tamba, in Brazil while she was visiting her parents. Jonathan and Tamba became AFLC missionaries in 1992. Their mission emphasis is planting churches. Jonathan is the son of Pastor John and Ruby Abel, AFLC Missionaries to Brazil.

Looking for Hope

By Tamba Abel

It was a hot, hot summer day in Southern Brazil as Maria Rosa trudged up the steep, winding road to the small village where she hoped to convince the storekeeper to give her some salt, sugar, and a few other necessary items for her kitchen, and to let her pay later. How tired and thirsty she was. Oh, she thought as she stopped for a brief rest, there must be more to life than this!

As she trudged on, tears ran down her cheeks, and she prayed, "God, if You exist, show Yourself to me."

Maria Rosa's life had always been hard. When she was just a little girl, her mother died. Since she was the oldest of her brothers and sisters, she had to take her mother's place in the home. Her father was a very angry man who often got drunk and treated his family badly. When Maria Rosa was a young woman, her father wanted her to marry a friend of his who was a widower. This man was twenty years older than Maria Rosa. She hated the thought of marrying this older man but wanted so badly to get out of her father's house that she agreed to marry Mr. Artur.

Though they had five children together, Mr. Artur and Maria Rosa did not love each other. Mr. Artur had a very hard time making a living, so they were always struggling to survive. The hope for a better life had brought them to where they were now, working for an older couple who had no children.

One day Maria Rosa and Mr. Artur heard that the government was giving out land in another part of the country, and they decided to move. As Maria Rosa gathered her children and prepared to get on the truck that would take them to a better life, the old lady she had worked for asked

Abby Ringdahl, age 9

Maria Rosa to leave her baby with her. She feared the child would die on the long trip. Her babe was so little—only a few months old. Maria Rosa knew that the woman was right. It would be a very hard trip.

As the truck started down the road, Maria Rosa looked back with tears falling down her cheeks. *Will I ever see my little one again?* she wondered.

Life in another part of the country proved to be harder than where they had lived before. This new land with steep hills and jungles had to be cleared by hand, which was a long and difficult process. They couldn't afford to buy seed, and since everything seemed so hopeless, Mr. Artur became very depressed. Maria Rosa didn't know how they would manage.

That's why she was on her way to the village—looking for food, looking for hope. And so she cried out, "There must be more to life than this! God, if You exist, show Yourself to me." Maria Rosa had been taught about God and had been told that she couldn't talk to Him herself. She thought she had to go through the Black Virgin Mary, Mary the mother of Jesus, the saints, or the priests. But now her heart's need was so desperate that she found herself calling out to God Himself.

Of course, God heard Maria Rosa, for He promises in His Word, "Call to Me and I will answer you, and I will tell you great and mighty things, which you do not know" (Jeremiah 33:3).

When she got to the village, she met missionaries John and Ruby Abel. Pastor John was preaching at special evangelistic services, and through his sharing of God's Word, Maria Rosa came to know Jesus as her personal Savior. Her cry for help was answered! In time, Mr. Artur, seeing the change in his wife, also received Christ as his Savior.

Soon life began to turn around for Maria and her husband. He was given a better job in the village, working at the highway weigh station. Over the years, the village grew into a small town, and Mr. Artur was put in charge of the waterworks. In this position, the mayor provided them with a large house. Before long, a Free Lutheran church was started in the area, and the couple became some of the first members. Maria opened her heart to serve others, and their home became a place for missionaries and Bible School students to stay. Maria Rosa delighted in praising the Lord and told others how God always supplied their needs.

Later, Maria Rosa and Mr. Artur moved to Campo Grande, Mato Grasso do Sul, Brazil. For three years, Maria Rosa prayed that someone would come to their town and establish a Free Lutheran congregation. The answer came when missionaries Jonathan and Tamba Abel were sent to start a church in that city.

There were more blessings from the Lord yet for Maria Rosa. In loving the Lord together, Maria Rosa and Mr. Artur learned to love one another. Maria Rosa cared for her husband tenderly in his last years. And the babe she left behind so many years before? Today, Edivaldo (eh-dee-VAHL-doo) lives only one block from her with his wife and children. Edivaldo had cared for the old couple who raised him from a baby until they passed away. Then he had sought to find his birth mother, Maria Rosa. Finding her, he also found the Lord.

Maria Rosa loves to tell her story. She shares the love of Jesus wherever she travels. She has learned that what the psalmist wrote is true: "Call upon Me in the day of trouble; I shall rescue you, and you will honor Me" (Psalm 50:15). Maria Rosa eagerly tells of how she was looking for hope and found Jesus.

QUESTIONS:
1. Why was Maria Rosa trudging up a steep road to the village?
2. Why had she left her baby behind with the old woman?
3. Who did Maria Rosa meet when she got to the village?
4. Talk about the ways God answered Maria Rosa's prayers.

Tamba (Wilkins) Abel was born in Mexicali, Mexico, to missionary parents. Soon they moved to Parana, Brazil, where Tamba grew up speaking Portuguese and being active in church work. While attending Bible college in Portland, Oregon, she made a trip to Brazil to visit her parents and met Jonathan Abel. After their marriage in 1985, they returned to the United States for further studies. In 1992 they became official missionaries with the AFLC. Their main concern is to plant churches.

Miracle on the Mountain

By Dan Giles

Dan was traveling through the mountains of Cañar, Ecuador. His friend Antonio's little daughter had just died, and Dan wanted to be with him to comfort him. He drove as far as he could, then parked his jeep on a wide spot on the dirt road, locked the door, and found the walking trail about fifty yards ahead.

Sometimes the trail was just a narrow path carved out of the side of a cliff. From a distance, the trails looked like eyebrows on the face of the mountain in the daylight. There was one place where the path turned sharply and went over a stone wall into a cornfield that was surrounded by sharp, thorny plants called "pincus." The path crossed the little cornfield, went through a wide opening in the cactus fence, and then continued to spiral down the valley before finally ending at the little house where Antonio and his family lived. "Thank You, Lord." Dan prayed as he arrived safely. "Give me Your words to help my friend."

About midnight it was time for Dan to leave. Antonio warned him, "Be careful! We heard some of the neighbors say that they were going to wait by the trail to kill you." Many of the neighbors hated the Christians, and especially the missionaries.

Dan knew that the Lord had promised to be with him wherever he went. He began to pray as he walked back up the mountain, "Please protect me, Lord!"

Dan followed the same trail as he had earlier that evening. When he reached the opening in the cactus fence, he went straight across the little cornfield to the exit on the other side. But when he got there, the opening was gone! It was completely hedged in by thick cactus plants! Dan walked around the inside of the field four times looking for the opening. It was really gone!

Suddenly, a man appeared out of the fog and walked across the field toward Dan. He was tall and slender and all dressed in white. He smiled.

"Hola, Meester!" he said. *"¿Qué hace usted por aqui?"* ("Hello, Mister. What are you doing here?")

"¡Buscando la salida!" ("Looking for the way out!") Dan replied.

"Follow me!" the man answered.

The man walked past Dan and continued across the field. When he got to the other side, the opening appeared! The man led Dan through the opening and kept walking. But instead of turning sharply to the right and following the trail, he went straight up the steep side of the mountain. He walked easily, as though he were on level ground. He didn't even seem to be breathing hard! Dan followed him the best that he could, grabbing rocks and trees to pull himself up the steep mountainside.

Corey Berge, age 15

When Dan got to the top, panting and gasping for air, the man was waiting for him. "Now I have to go this way," he smiled, pointing to the left. "But you should go that way." He pointed down the trail to the right. Exhausted from the climb, Dan nodded. "Okay!" he gasped. Dan started down the trail, then suddenly thought, I should thank him for helping me! He turned around to say "thank you," but the man was gone! There was no one there! Dan looked carefully around him and then down at the trail. In the dirt there was only one set of footprints—his own!

By now Dan was pretty sure who the stranger was. "Thank You, Lord," he prayed. "You always keep Your promises." Remembering a promise the Lord had given him, he said it to himself once again: "They [the angels] will bear you up in their hands, that you do not strike your foot against a stone" (Psalm 91:12).

Dan started down the trail, following the way the man in white had told him to go. After a while, he came to a place where the trail had been washed out by a landslide. Dan could see that the trail continued on the other side, but it was too far for him to jump across. He tried to see how deep the chasm was, but he couldn't see the bottom. He found a little rock and tossed it down into the dark to see if he could tell how deep it was, but he never even heard it hit bottom!

Dan thought, if that was who I think it was, and he told me to go this way, I should do what he says! "Okay, Lord, You promised!" he exclaimed, and he stepped out over the seemingly bottomless gully.

His foot seemed to hit something solid, just like a concrete sidewalk. He looked down in amazement but couldn't see anything. Was it an invisible sidewalk? Trembling with amazement at what he was doing, he walked across to the other side.

As he got closer to the car, he could hear the voices of the men who were waiting to kill him. He could hear them plotting, and he realized that they were waiting for him on the wrong trail! Because Dan had followed the mysterious man in white up the mountain, and because he had followed his directions and stepped out on thin air over that deep gully, he had come out at a different place. He found himself behind the jeep instead of ahead of it where the men were waiting.

Dan quietly slipped up behind the jeep, got inside, and released the brake. He rolled backwards down the mountain until he was far enough away to turn around, start the motor, and drive home.

"Thank You, Lord," he breathed. "Your angels really lifted me up today!"

QUESTIONS:
1. Why did Antonio warn Dan to be careful as he walked back down the mountain?
2. Why couldn't Dan get out of the cornfield?
3. Who do you think appeared to Dan in the middle of the field, all dressed in white, to guide him out?
4. What promise from God's Word did Dan remember?
5. How did the angels "lift him up" in their hands that night?

Dan Giles and his wife, Debbie, met at California Lutheran Bible School. They studied under the Summer Institute of Linguistics at the University of North Dakota and the University of Texas, Arlington. They then served with All Nations Frontier Mission under the World Mission Prayer League in Ecuador from 1978-1981. They returned to the U.S., and Dan entered the Association Free Lutheran Theological Seminary, graduating in 1985. They were commissioned shortly thereafter as AFLC missionaries to Mexico where they served until 2008.

Irma, God's Messenger of Contentment

By Richard Gunderson

The black clouds were hanging low over the village of Apolo. Looking out the window toward the airstrip, Dick's heart felt heavy, so heavy. Turning to his wife, he sighed, "It doesn't look like the plane will get in today either."

"I know," she answered. "Today is the ninth day of this bad weather. Nine days of waiting for the children to come. Nine days of rain, rain, rain!"

It was just a few days before Christmas, and the three Gunderson children were not yet home for the holidays. They attended Carachipampa (kah-rah-CHEE-pahm-pah), a missionary children's boarding school just outside the city of Cochabamba (COH-chah-bahm-bah), Bolivia, in South America. There hadn't been any problem for them to get to LaPaz from the school. The weather didn't interfere with the ten-hour train ride up the mountains, but flying into Apolo in a small plane under these conditions was another matter.

"You know, it might as well be half a world away instead of just an hour's flight," Dick complained, sitting down beside his wife, Clara. If only they hadn't taken this assignment in this remote village, the family would have been together for the whole school vacation. As it was, ten days had already gone by.

They sat in the midst of the darkening day with heaviness of heart, talking over the situation and trying to pray, but complaining to each other and feeling sorry for themselves too. Didn't the Lord know that the children needed to be with them? Weren't they here to do God's work of ministering to others? They had sent the children to boarding school because they felt it was the very best choice for a good education. They hadn't expected to have an impossible situation like this.

The couple fell silent, wrapped up in their own thoughts and emotions. The house they were living in was right up against the road, and as the silence inside the house lengthened, the chatter outside became evident. The mild temperatures in this lowland village didn't necessitate glass in the windows, and so the voices of two young girls coming down the street could be heard clearly.

"Irma, conoces tú algo acerca del helados?" (Irma, do you know anything about ice cream?")

"Sí, cómo no!" ("Yes, of course!") Irma responded.

"Cómo es que tú conoces helados?" ("How is it that you know about ice cream?") Irma's friend asked.

"Bueno, fui a LaPaz visitando a mi abuela. Ella me llevó a una heladaría y me compró un helado." ("Well, I went to LaPaz to visit my grandmother, and she took me to an ice cream shop and bought me an ice cream cone.")

Malena Twedt, age 4

"Irma, cómo fue el sabor?" ("Irma, how did it taste?")

Irma then enthusiastically began to tell her friend that it was cool, sweet, rich in flavor, and delicious. It was the very best thing she had ever tasted!

The conversation faded as the girls walked on down the street. But Dick had heard enough for him to realize how very selfish he was. An important truth broke through to him as he sat in the darkening living room: Why is it that some people can find happiness in something as insignificant as ice cream? What does it take to make me happy and content?

"Clara," he said, "hearing Irma tell her friend about the joy of eating ice cream has shown me that I have been so selfish thinking about myself and not having the kids here."

"I know. I feel it too," she answered. "Just because we're here in another country, doing God's work, do we always expect everything to go the way we want it to go? Why can't we be content with what God has given us? Let's get the Bible and read the verse in Hebrews that God gave to us when He called us here to Bolivia."

Dick went to his desk and brought the Bible back to the living room. He turned to Hebrews 13:5 and read, "Let your character be free from the love of money and be content with what you have, for He Himself has said, 'I WILL NEVER DESERT YOU, NOR WILL I EVER FORSAKE YOU.'"

"Oh, I'm so glad you thought about reading that verse right now!" Dick said. "The children are in His care, too, and we can trust Him. God has spoken to me so clearly right now, confirming that we are in His will serving Him, and He will take care of what we need and what our children need."

Together they bowed in prayer, thanking the Lord for His Word to them and for His presence with them and with their children.

And the children? Christine, Daniel, and Peder arrived in the afternoon of December 24. The plane was seen by the villagers as it appeared to swoop down through a break in the clouds. Everyone—Dick and Clara included—ran to the airstrip, excited, giddy with the joy of welcoming their loved ones who were so long overdue.

A wonderful Christmas was theirs as they joined together with other Christians to celebrate the birth of the babe, Jesus, who left His home in heaven to come to earth as God's great gift, to be the Savior of all.

QUESTIONS:
1. Can you think of a time you received a gift that made you want to tell others about it?
2. Why was it so easy for Irma to tell her friend about ice cream?
3. Have you ever felt sorry for yourself because something didn't go the way you wanted it to go? How did the Lord help you?
4. What does the word "content" mean? What makes you happy and content?

Richard Gunderson graduated from the Association Free Lutheran Theological Seminary in 1967. He and his family served under the World Mission Prayer League in Bolivia from 1967-1976 and in Mexico from 1977-1983 and again in 1994-2000. He served churches in Brooten, Minnesota; Escanaba, Michigan; and Lake Stevens, Washington, on a full-time basis and has served several other congregations on an interim basis. He currently teaches part-time at AFLBS and serves as Assistant to the AFLC President. He and his wife, Clara, are members of Sunnyside Free Lutheran Church in Stacy, Minnesota.

Christmas in Bolivia

By Clara Gunderson

"Children, children, come and listen as I tell you a story about following Jesus and being His disciple," said Mrs. Jones one Sunday morning. She and her family had recently returned to Minneapolis after spending several years in the country of Bolivia. Bolivia is in South America, and they had been missionaries to the Aymara (eye-MAH-rah) people there who live high in the Andes Mountains.

Now she was back in their home church, eager to tell everyone all about their experiences—eager to tell the children this morning of how Jesus had helped her when she was feeling very lonesome and unhappy.

She started by telling the group of boys and girls that going to a faraway country can be very hard. It was hard, she told them, because she hadn't known the language the people spoke. They spoke Spanish and another hard language called "Aymara." It had been difficult because it was strange to see how they dressed. The men and boys wore knit hats that came down over their ears, ponchos or blankets on their backs, and rubber sandals on their feet. The ladies and girls wore wide skirts, embroidered blouses, and hats on their heads, and they, too, wore ponchos on their backs. It had been hard, she told them, because they ate food she wasn't used to with different tastes she'd never had before.

Because they had arrived in December, she had expected to see Christmas decorations on the streets and in the stores, homes with bright lights, and decorated trees showing through the windows. But no, there hadn't been any of this! She had not seen one manger scene. Instead, the houses were all set behind high walls. The stores had only a few items on display, and many did not even have display windows. When they went into business offices, she was surprised how drab they were. There were no wall decorations, and there was nothing to remind you that Jesus' birth was soon to be celebrated.

Even worse, she had been terribly lonesome for her own mother and father, her sisters, cousins, aunts, and uncles. The years preparing to go to Bolivia had been busy, and money wasn't plentiful, but they had always managed to get home for the holidays. Now, she had thought, I don't feel at home, and I hate it that there are no signs of Christmas here. Doesn't anyone care?

"Oh," said Mrs. Jones to the children, "I had so much to learn! The Lord showed me in many ways how closed my heart was, how closed my mind was to this new country and to the people around me. I didn't see their beauty. I only saw dark skin, dark eyes, and black hair!"

She went on to tell them that as the days passed, she started to realize that although the outward signs of Christmas were not there, she had seen her fellow-missionaries (their children's new "aunts and "uncles"), making special preparations to be with the different churches. Some were practicing with a group of young people for a play they would present. Others were preparing treats to serve. One missionary family was wrapping small gifts to give to the children in one of the country churches.

When Christmas Eve finally arrived, she and her family had gone to church with some of the other missionaries. As they entered, she saw a beautiful scene! Long evergreen needles covered the entire floor, sending up a wonderful fragrance. Spanish moss hung in swags across the ceiling. Live flowers of several colors adorned the walls. Familiar Christmas carols were sung in the beautiful new language, and for the very first time she heard the Christmas story in another language, the one she would come to know very well. And the children! Why, their faces were glowing with the excitement of the evening and the anticipation of the treats to come. It had been no different, really, from the excitement of her own children—Cristina, Danny, and Peder—at Christmastime.

Arriving back at the mission home later that evening, Mrs. Jones continued, there had been presents under the tree for her family. They were gifts, no doubt, that had been prepared beforehand by her fellow-missionaries, while she had only been thinking of herself and how lonesome she was. Later, a Bolivian family had stopped by to wish them a *"Feliz Navidad"* (Merry Christmas) and to leave a package of holiday treats. How quickly, how gently, the Lord had helped her in her loneliness.

"You know," she told the children, "being Jesus' disciple and following Him can be hard, but He always remembers His promises. The promise He gave me before leaving for Bolivia is found in Hebrews 13:5: "Make sure that your character is free from the love of money, being content with what you have; for He Himself has said, 'I WILL NEVER LEAVE YOU, NOR WILL I EVER FORSAKE YOU.'"

Then she added, "That Christmas I learned to be open to the Bolivian people—open to their ways, to their food, and to everything that made them God's children. I realized also that there had been no colored lights or shiny balls on the trees in Bethlehem the night Jesus was born—just a tiny babe in a manger."

Abigail Kangas, age 4

QUESTIONS:
1. Why was Mrs. Jones unhappy?
2. What was different about Christmas in Bolivia?
3. What did the Lord teach Mrs. Jones?
4. What can you learn from Hebrews 13:5? How can it be an encouragement to you?

"Mrs. Jones" in this story is Clara Gunderson. Clara and her family served in Bolivia under the World Mission Prayer League (WMPL) from 1967-1976. They also served under WMPL in Mexico for eleven years. Her husband, Richard, graduated from the Association Free Lutheran Theological Seminary in 1967 and today serves as Assistant to the President of the AFLC. They are members of Sunnyside Free Lutheran Church, Stacy, Minnesota.

Pronunciation Key

Phonetic Symbol	Example	Used in Text
ä	ah	as in ball
ĕ	eh	as in pet
ō	oh	as in boat
ĭ	ih	as in hit
ŭ	uh	as in cut
ē	ee	as in heel
o͞o	oo	as in pool
ā	ay	as in day
ă	a	as in cat
ī	i	as in bike

Story Illustrators

Name	Age	City	State
Abel, April	16	Maringa	Paraná, Brazil
Ackerman, Elise	9	Harrisburg	South Dakota
Ackerman, Lydia	6	Harrisburg	South Dakota
Ackerman, Ross	10	Harrisburg	South Dakota
Anderson, Kaelyn	13	Bagley	Minnesota
Anderson, Sarah	10	Bagley	Minnesota
Belinski, Kayla	15	Newark	Illinois
Berge, Corey	15	Maple Grove	Minnesota
Berntson, April	11	Valley City	North Dakota
Berntson, Bethany	12	Valley City	North Dakota
Berntson, Jacob	9	Valley City	North Dakota
Berntson, Hunter	8	Buffalo	North Dakota
Berntson, Levi	12	Buffalo	North Dakota
Bowman, Helen	16	Newark	Illinois
Cardiges, Alexia	9	South Park	Pennsylvania
Dryburgh, Grace	7	Grafton	North Dakota
Dryburgh, Rachel	12	Grafton	North Dakota
Erickson, Tyler	12	Roseau	Minnesota
Haglin, Cassie	14	Munich	North Dakota
Haug, Elijah	17	Brooklyn Park	Minnesota
Horn, Andrew	16	Kenyon	Minnesota
Jameson, Rebecca	11	Earlville	Illinois

Appendix B

Name	Age	City	State
Jones, Ryan	11	New Hope	Minnesota
Kangas, Abigail	4	Solon Springs	Wisconsin
Mairs, Bethany	8	Plymouth	Minnesota
Mairs, Morgan	13	Plymouth	Minnesota
Peterson, David	7	Valley City	North Dakota
Peterson, Hannah	10	Valley City	North Dakota
Peterson, Rebekah	11	Valley City	North Dakota
Quanbeck, Andrew	14	Minot	North Dakota
Quanbeck, Luke	16	Minot	North Dakota
Rassi, Jorgie	7	Plymouth	Minnesota
Reynolds, Nicholas	11	Stanley	North Dakota
Ringdahl, Abby	9	Wahpeton	North Dakota
Ringdahl, Jack	6	Wahpeton	North Dakota
Schram, Erin	17	Thief River Falls	Minnesota
Twedt, Emma	13	Oxbow	North Dakota
Twedt, Malena	4	Portland	North Dakota
Twedt, Solveig	9	Portland	North Dakota
Unverzagt, Emma	9	Sparta	Wisconsin
Unverzagt, Sigre	11	Sparta	Wisconsin
Unverzagt, Zofeyah	6	Sparta	Wisconsin
Welsch, Susan	17	Amery	Wisconsin

Teaching Missions to Children

*"I am sending you, to open their eyes
so that they may turn from darkness to light."*
Acts 26:17-18

As children hear about missionaries around the world, they will learn many things that may be different about living in another country. But they will also see that all people have one thing in common: We all need Jesus as our Savior! Children can be encouraged to pray for others and to be missionaries for Christ wherever they are.

Mission Club
Meet once a month after school to teach about missions. Include mission stories and letters from missionaries and do handcrafts and service projects. Talk about how students can be missionaries every day right where they are.

Bulletin Board Map
Cover a bulletin board with a large map of the world. Mount photos of missionaries around the edges of the map. Run yarn from the pictures to the countries where the missionaries serve. Pray for these missionaries regularly in church and Sunday School.

Greeting Cards
Send birthday, Christmas, and other special day cards to missionaries. Encourage children to send cards to missionary children their own age.

Exchange Recordings
Record favorite songs and memory verses or tell about what you are studying in Sunday School. Send the recording to a missionary family and ask questions about their church and Sunday School.

Support a Missionary
Select a specific missionary to take an offering for once a month. Keep students regularly informed about the mission work.

Foreign Student
Sponsor a foreign student individually or as a church. Have the student stay with a family from your church. You will learn much about the country and culture he or she comes from and can also share the love of Jesus through your words and actions.

Communication
If you have a ham radio operator in your church, ask him to make contact with a missionary. Let the students talk with the missionary. Other communication options include contact through email, video, or webcam.

Book Reports
Have students read a book about a missionary. Then ask them to give an oral report to the rest of the class.

Drama
Dramatize a scene from the life of a missionary from one of the books students have read.

Missionary Conference
Invite missionaries to tell of their work and show videos or slides. Have each class be responsible for planning a different part of the conference (Scripture readings, prayer sessions, music, food, displays).

Prayer Wheel
Cut a large circle out of colored paper. Draw lines dividing into equal sections. Label each section with a missionary and a missions Bible verse. Cut another circle the same size with a wedge-shaped window and fasten over the top of the first circle. Turn the wheel to one section each week. Encourage children to use their Missionary Prayer Wheel for personal prayer and memorization.

Music in a Foreign Language
Teach a translation of a Christian song such as "Jesus Loves Me."

Who Am I?
After your class has learned about several missionaries, have a "Who Am I?" quiz using two or three missionaries each week. Give clues as to the missionary's identity, allowing the children time to guess between each clue.

Mission Field Study
Have students look for news articles about a specific mission field. Collect various materials that are made in that country. Create a display of the materials. Have pupils explain about the items they have brought. Locate the country on the map. Ask students to research specific facts. What is the population? What are the people like? What kind of food do they eat? How do they dress? What do they believe about God? What is the climate like? Have each class volunteer to find out answers to specific questions during the next week. Each week, allow a few minutes for students to share information they have learned. For example, news articles, reading missionary letters, giving prayer suggestions, etc.

Special Needs
Contact a missionary to find out specific needs. Have students collect some of the items requested. Pack up the box together and send to the missionary.

Visit a Mission Field
Take a trip to a mission "field" to observe the work and how people live. Volunteer to come and help with projects or other needs.

Resource File
Help students collect information on various mission fields and store in a resource file or a loose-leaf notebook. Choose one mission field to study each month.

Missionary Bracelet/Key Fob/Zipper-pull
Using alphabet beads, string the names of individual missionaries or countries onto a 7-9" cord. Tie a clasp onto each end of the cord. Let participants select a bracelet to wear for a week and pray for that missionary. The following week, the bracelet can be traded for a different one with a different name. (Idea may be modified for use as a key fob or zipper-pull.)